Scripture — God's Handbook for Evangelizing

Catholics seeking confidence and the skills to be effective witnesses to the Gospel will find *Scripture — God's Handbook for Evangelizing Catholics* a welcome and inspiring tool for reading the Gospel with the mind of the church and learning how to listen, reflect, and respond to God's Word. This book is tailor-made for those who are looking for a way to accept the challenge of the New Evangelization.

✠ *Cardinal Donald Wuerl, Archbishop of Washington*

Pope Francis has called the New Evangelization a "witness of joy." This book explores this witness of joy by tapping the long and rich tradition of the Catholic Church, which over the centuries has celebrated heroes of evangelization to be learned from and imitated. Stephen Binz imparts this confident joy in a very engaging and readable fashion.

✠ *Joseph E. Kurtz, Archbishop of Louisville,*
President of the United States Conference of Catholic Bishops

In this book, Stephen Binz brings together the themes of the past two general synods of bishops, the "Word of God" and the "New Evangelization," in a wonderfully creative and life-giving way that opens new horizons for the church. This is required reading for all those who are concerned with the future of our Church and its mission to bring the Good News to all.

✠ *Paul-André Durocher, Archbishop of Gatineau,*
President of the Canadian Conference of Catholic Bishops

Stephen Binz provides a most welcome contribution to the New Evangelization. He convincingly and effectively shows that because the New Evangelization is about encountering the person of Jesus, its necessary foundation resides in the Scriptures as the Word of God. For anyone looking for an easily accessible text that demonstrates the essential connection between Scripture and the New Evangelization, this is for them.

✠ *Blase J. Cupich, Bishop of Spokane*

This imminently practical and accessible book from Stephen Binz makes an important contribution to the area of Scripture and the New

Evangelization. Introducing readers to the sacred art of lectio divina, the principle that those who learn to listen to the word of God will learn to witness to the word of God is explored through the Scriptures, the lives of the saints, and the Blessed Mother.

✠ *David L. Ricken, Bishop of Green Bay*

In this book, Stephen Binz has provided a new perspective on both the exercise of lectio divina and the goal of New Evangelization. To the traditional four steps of *lectio*, he adds witness — faithful living in Christ. The many years he has been engaged in and written about lectio divina have been brought to fruition in this book.

Dianne Bergant, Catholic Theological Union, Chicago

This book is a compelling demonstration of the link between Scripture and the New Evangelization. Through biblical examples and the lives of the saints, Stephen Binz shows how Catholics can become effective witnesses to the Word by first being prayerful hearers of the Word. A great tool for forming "evangelical Catholics" of the third millennium.

Mary Healy, Associate Professor of Sacred Scripture at Sacred Heart Major Seminary, coeditor of the Catholic Commentary on Sacred Scripture

Stephen Binz helps the reader to put the Gospel at the center of the "New Evangelization," which is good news indeed! Rooted in Scripture, guided by history, and directed by the prayer of lectio divina, this book offers the church a resource and firm foundation for thinking about evangelization in the twenty-first century.

Daniel P. Horan, O.F.M., Franciscan friar,
Holy Name Province, author

Scripture is a privileged place to encounter God. Yet for some Catholics the Bible remains confusing, overwhelming, or even off-limits — the province of other Christian denominations. But with this marvelous invitation to unlock the riches of the Old and New Testaments, Stephen J. Binz shows us what it means for Catholics to read the Bible "expectantly," secure in the knowledge that this is where God desires to encounter us. A terrific resource for anyone who wishes to experience — or invite others to experience — the Living Word.

James Martin, S.J., author, The Colbert Report *chaplain,*
and editor at America *magazine*

Stephen Binz draws on his deep knowledge of Scripture and the Catholic Tradition to give us an inspiring and helpful guide for the new evangelization. Solid. Recommended.

Ralph Martin, Director of Graduate Theology Programs in the
New Evangelization, Sacred Heart Major Seminary, Archdiocese of Detroit

Stephen Binz masterfully weaves Scripture with themes from the New Evangelization and makes a very significant contribution to the church's evangelizing and catechizing efforts. This work is an inspiring and an engaging resource for encountering Jesus afresh. It is sure to renew spirits, transform lives, and set hearts on fire with the Gospel story and commitment to share the Good News.

Sr. Edith Prendergast, Director of Religious Education,
Archdiocese of Los Angeles

As Catholics, we are all called to participate in the New Evangelization, but that can be somewhat intimidating for even the most devoted among us. Now, thanks to Stephen Binz, we have a much-needed guide to show us the way. Using examples of saints, spiritual traditions, and the ancient practice of lectio divina, he teaches us how to go from Word to witness by allowing sacred Scripture to serve as both anchor and compass.

Mary DeTurris Poust, columnist, journalist, and author

Stephen Binz writes fine books for an audience hungry for spiritual meaning based on solid Catholic teaching, principles, and practice. This book is unique in that it blends Scripture with the lives of the saints, the call for a "new evangelization," and the ancient form of prayer known as lectio divina.

Brian Schmisek, Director of the Institute of Pastoral Studies,
Loyola University Chicago

With all the hallmarks of an experienced writer whose work is geared toward the "person in the pew," Stephen Binz has produced a lovely guide to both encourage and equip Catholics to be effective bearers of God's Word. At the heart of this work is a belief I also share, "The more we become biblical Catholics, the more we will become evangelizing Catholics." Renewing God's people and inviting others to experience Christ is a lifelong call and mission that is embodied in the lives of those who populate the pages of our Bible and the generations of our history as a people. This volume will help us all to appreciate our place in the continuing evolution of salvation history.

Catherine Upchurch, Director of Little Rock Scripture Study

According to the recent Synod on the New Evangelization, the Bible "should permeate homilies, catechesis, and every effort to pass on the faith." It's the ground of effective evangelization, as Stephen Binz knows. For decades he's helped Catholics to read and love the Bible. In his newest and most important book, though, he unlocks its evangelizing power. You'll discover how reading Scripture equips you to share its message and how saints throughout history evangelized with the Bible. Read this book and you'll become a potent evangelist yourself.

Brandon Vogt, Content Director at Word on Fire

In this inviting and accessible text, Stephen Binz urges readers to move toward more meaningful contemplation of and commitment to the Word. He offers the tools and encouragement needed not only to grow in relationship with Christ but to more fully engage with the world as people of God.

Kerry Weber, author, managing editor at America *magazine*

Prolific author Stephen Binz explains how the ancient practice of lectio divina can aid the "New Evangelization." In fact, he shows how intimately the Bible is related to *all* evangelization, a view I heartily endorse. Interested readers, whether individuals or study groups, will find this book a reliable guide.

Ronald D. Witherup, S.S., Superior General of the Sulpicians, Paris

This is an important book. Stephen Binz knows that we can't convert the world until we've been converted ourselves. It's not just a matter of Church membership. We need to be shaped by the Word of God. So he teaches us to hear the Word, trust it, understand it, and be transformed by it. Only then can we share it with others and reach them effectively. He also shows us how this process worked in the lives of the saints and how it can make us saints too. Evangelization is part of the mission of God's people in the Old Testament and the New. It's your mission and mine. It begins now — and finds a very good beginning in these pages.

Scott Hahn, President of the St. Paul Center for Biblical Theology

Scripture

God's Handbook
for Evangelizing
Catholics

Scripture

God's Handbook for Evangelizing Catholics

STEPHEN J. BINZ

Our Sunday Visitor Publishing Division
Our Sunday Visitor, Inc.
Huntington, Indiana 46750

Nihil Obstat:
Msgr. Michael Heintz, Ph.D.
Censor Librorum

Imprimatur:
✠ Kevin C. Rhoades
Bishop of Fort Wayne-South Bend
October 7, 2013

The *Nihil Obstat* and *Imprimatur* are declarations that a work is free from doctrinal or moral error. It is not implied that those who have granted the *Nihil Obstat* and *Imprimatur* agree with the contents, opinions, or statements expressed.

Scripture citations used in this work are taken from the *New Revised Standard Version Bible: Catholic Edition*, copyright © 1989, 1993 National Council of the Churches of Christ in the United States of America. Used by permission. All rights reserved.

English translation of the *Catechism of the Catholic Church* for use in the United States of America copyright © 1994, United States Catholic Conference, Inc. — Libreria Editrice Vaticana. English translation of the *Catechism of the Catholic Church: Modifications from the Editio Typica* copyright © 1997, United States Catholic Conference, Inc. — Libreria Editrice Vaticana.

Quotations from papal and other Vatican-generated documents available on vatican.va are copyright © Libreria Editrice Vaticana.

Every reasonable effort has been made to determine copyright holders of excerpted materials and to secure permissions as needed. If any copyrighted materials have been inadvertently used in this work without proper credit being given in one form or another, please notify Our Sunday Visitor in writing so that future printings of this work may be corrected accordingly.

ISBN 978-1-61278-701-5 (Inventory No. T1406)
eISBN: 978-1-61278-340-6
LCCN: 2014940416

Cover design: Tyler Ottinger
Cover image: iStock Photo

PRINTED IN THE UNITED STATES OF AMERICA

TABLE OF CONTENTS

Foreword by Joseph E. Kurtz, Archbishop of Louisville   13

Preface   15

Recovering the Evangelical Dimension of Catholicism

CHAPTER 1

The Word of God and the New Evangelization   21

Hearing God's Word Anew through Lectio Divina   24

Witnessing to God's Word through the
New Evangelization   27

Obstructions to Hearing and Witnessing
God's Word Today   29

Becoming Evangelical Catholics   35

For Reflection or Discussion   39

CHAPTER 2

Evangelizing Moments in Catholic History   41

St. Paul of Tarsus   42

St. Benedict of Nursia   44

St. Francis of Assisi   47

St. Dominic of Guzman   50

St. Ignatius of Loyola   54

St. Thérèse of Lisieux   57

The Word of God in the New Evangelization   60

For Reflection or Discussion   61

CHAPTER 3

Reading the Bible as Evangelizing Catholics   63

1) Listen for the Voice of God   65

2) Trust in God's Inspiration   66

3) Understand the One Story of Salvation   70

4) Discover the Book of Christ   73

5) Search for Beauty   76

6) Experience Scripture with Your Whole Self   *79*
7) Develop a Biblical Imagination   *81*
8) Read with Expectation   *84*
9) Celebrate the Word in Union with the Sacraments   *87*
10) Expect to Become an Evangelizer   *91*
For Reflection or Discussion   *93*

Evangelization at the Heart of Sacred Scripture

CHAPTER 4
Evangelization in Ancient Israel   *97*

God Forms Israel as a People with a Divine Mission   *98*
From Twelve United Tribes to a People Dispersed among
   the Nations   *101*
The Prophets Call God's People to Be Witnesses
   to the Peoples of the Earth   *105*
From Messianic Hope to the Christian Gospel   *111*
For Reflection or Discussion   *112*

CHAPTER 5
Evangelization in the Gospels   *113*

Announcing the Kingdom of God   *114*
Israel Gathered for Its Mission to the Nations   *116*
Witnesses of a New Creation Formed in the Death and
   Resurrection of Jesus   *118*
Jesus Calls His Disciples to Evangelize   *120*
For Reflection or Discussion   *125*

CHAPTER 6
Evangelization in the Apostolic Church   *127*

The Holy Spirit Impels the Church to Evangelize   *128*
The Mission of Peter and Paul   *131*
Evangelization in the Letters of the New Testament   *136*
For Reflection or Discussion   *142*

Evangelizing the Church and the World through Sacred Scripture

CHAPTER 7
Becoming Communities of the Word   145

Catholic Bible Study for the Third Millennium   145
Taking Away the Obstacles to Growth   148
Studying the Book of the Church   151
Other Ways of Forming Communities of the Word   154
Reading the Bible Anew   155
For Reflection or Discussion   159

CHAPTER 8
Lectio Divina for Evangelization   161

Listening — Reading the Text with Expectation   163
Meditation — Reflecting on the Meaning
    and Message of the Text   165
Praying — Responding to God's Word
    from the Heart   166
Contemplation — Quietly Resting in God   168
Witness — Faithful Living in Christ   170
Evangelizers as Contemplative Witnesses   172
For Reflection or Discussion   175

CHAPTER 9
Woman of the Word and Star of the New
Evangelization   177

Hearing the Word of God and Doing It   177
Mary in the Mysteries of the Gospel   179
Mary as Exemplar of Lectio Divina   184
Star of the New Evangelization   186
With Mary to Jesus   188
For Reflection or Discussion   189

Foreword

I recall someone telling me how he ended up volunteering for a local nonprofit. He recounted: "At Friday football games my friend spoke with such energy and joy about his involvement in that organization that I said to myself, 'You have to find out what gives him such joy!' And I did, and here I am volunteering." This vignette captures the spirit of the New Evangelization — what Pope Francis has called a "witness of joy" — that is evident in a life well grounded in the good news of Jesus Christ.

Sadly, the caricature of this witnessing too frequently conveys a hectic, preachy quality that one does with little preparation. Instead, *Scripture — God's Handbook for Evangelizing Catholics* explores this witness of joy by tapping the long and rich tradition of the Catholic Church, which over the centuries has celebrated heroes of evangelization to be learned from and imitated.

The Synod on the New Evangelization for the Transmission of Faith, held in Rome in October of 2012, uses the word "serene" to describe the new evangelizer. A long way from hectic and unprepared, the serene person taps that long tradition captured by a phrase from St. Thomas Aquinas, now the theme of the Dominicans: "*Contemplare et contemplata aliis tradere*" — to contemplate and share the fruit of that contemplation with others.

When Jesus sent out his disciples as missioners of the good news, they had the joy that comes from an encounter with the Son of God, the Word. It is this confident joy that Stephen Binz imparts in a very engaging and readable fashion.

The author uses the phrase "expectant reading." We need to be prepared and hopeful — and this handbook leads us through the preparation in some exciting ways. Borrowing his analogy, it is not a good idea to toss the car keys to an unprepared teen and say, "Go, drive." Being prepared requires meeting the Lord Jesus in and through Sacred Scripture and being rooted in the apostolic tradition. Thus, there is a way to read Sacred Scripture that is deeply Catholic.

Using a variety of modes that are part of the rich tapestry of spiritual reading and meditation over the centuries, Stephen provides summary examples to fit every size. These are the "hero evangelizers" through the ages — from St. Paul and his big missionary journeys to the Little Flower, St. Thérèse of Lisieux, with her Little Way. Digging even deeper into Sacred Scripture, he identifies announcers of joy from the Old Testament and, of course, the Samaritan woman at the well who thirsts, encounters Jesus, and then can't stop telling others about him.

Being rooted in the apostolic tradition means reading within a community called the church, for Sacred Scripture is not meant to isolate one in individualistic interpretation. Stephen has a great summary phrase: "The Eucharistic liturgy won't let us read the Bible individualistically."

"Expectant reading" means approaching Sacred Scripture with a humble conviction that the Holy Spirit will speak to the heart of the listener. This expectation forms the framework for the various methods of approaching God's word deeply rooted in Catholic tradition. They all have in common the "encounter with the Lord Jesus" that forms the core of all true evangelization.

The first words of Vatican Council II's *Constitution on Divine Revelation* are quoted by the author and yield the best summary of the entire book: "Hearing the word of God with reverence and proclaiming it with faith." Whether this book is read privately or used as a tool for small group formation, it will yield great preparation for the work at hand: sharing with a world thirsting for the witness to joy that results from our encounter with the Lord Jesus in and through the church.

Most Reverend Joseph E. Kurtz, D.D., Archbishop of Louisville

Preface

For the past thirty years, my work has been engaged in helping Catholics read the Bible. I began preparing for this work through graduate work in biblical studies in light of the Second Vatican Council document *Dei Verbum*, which states that "access to sacred Scripture ought to be open wide to the Christian faithful" (*DV*, 22) and exhorts all the faithful "to learn 'the surpassing knowledge of Jesus Christ' (Phil 3:8) by frequent reading of the divine Scriptures" (*DV*, 25). Through teaching and writing, developing programs, and publishing books, I've sought to make access to Scripture a bit more open to Catholics and to enable that "frequent reading" urged by the Council.

One of the great things I've discovered through my personal experience and biblical ministry is the transformative effects of Scripture on our lives. Through reading Scripture, we become more centered on Jesus, living our lives more intimately in him. Especially as we learn how to read Scripture as the word of God, we become more personally engaged in discipleship and living our lives more consciously focused on the Lord. In this way we become evangelized Catholics — people whose lives are rooted in the gospel — and we become evangelizing Catholics — whose lives reflect the gospel to others and lead others to faith.

In recent years my work has focused on helping people read Scripture through the sacred art of lectio divina. The various study series I have written use this ancient method to help Christians to read and study the Bible in a transformative way that leads them to reflection, prayer, contemplation, and witness. I have discovered that it is not just "frequent reading" that transforms lives and engages us as disciples. Rather, it is expectant reading, the kind of reading encouraged by lectio divina. When we are fully convinced that the same Spirit who inspired Scripture also works within us as we read, we trust that God is going to renew us from within and empower us to mission as we listen to and reflect upon his word.

I have become convinced that this evangelizing power of the word of God must be the foundation of the New Evangelization. If God's people are to be authentic evangelizers, we must be continually nourished by Scripture and allow its transforming power to renew our lives and make us living witnesses to God's kingdom for others. My thinking and teaching about this connection has been particularly influenced by our recent Popes: John Paul II, Benedict XVI, and Francis. Their clarion call to the New Evangelization and its necessary connection to the word of God, especially as embodied in the teachings of the Synods on the Word of God and on the New Evangelization, have empowered my research for this book.

The recent work of Evangelical Christians has also influenced my thoughts on the essential relationship between the Bible and the mission of evangelization. I recently participated in a conference at the Newbigin House of Studies in San Francisco on Leadership for the Church-in-Mission. The keynote presentations by N. T. Wright, addressing representatives of over a dozen Christian denominations, helped me to perceive the broad movement of God's Spirit in this regard throughout the people of God. I have been particularly fascinated by the excellent theological works of Christopher J.H. Wright, Michael W. Goheen, Arthur F. Glasser, William J. Abraham, Bryan Stone, and Richard Bauckham, and certainly the foundational work and witness of Lesslie Newbigin and John Stott.

I also recently participated in a continuing seminar of the Catholic Biblical Association of America at the University of Notre Dame. The discussion centered on *Verbum Domini* and the New Evangelization with the aim of sharing our reflections with the Synod of Bishops. Insightful presentations included those by Peter S. Williamson, Mary Healy, Ronald D. Witherup, Bishop Michael Byrnes, and Thomas Osborne, representing the worldwide Catholic Biblical Federation. Since that meeting, I have been enriched through reading the work of Cardinal Rino Fisichella, President of the Pontifical Council for New Evangelization; Cardinal Avery Dulles, S.J.; Cardinal Francis George, O.M.I.; Cardinal Donald Wuerl, and Father Robert Barron. Their masterful reflections on the New Evangelization are rooted in Scripture and have helped me understand the close relationship of the two.

Fortuitously, I was completing this book as Pope Francis issued his apostolic exhortation *Evangelii Gaudium* ("The Joy of the Gospel"), which reinforces the ideas of this work and of my biblical ministry. In #175, he insists that "the study of the sacred Scriptures must be a door opened to every believer." Furthermore, he states,

"Evangelization demands familiarity with God's word, which calls for dioceses, parishes, and Catholic associations to provide for a serious, ongoing study of the Bible, while encouraging its prayerful individual and communal reading." No other papal teaching could possibly encourage me more to continue doing the work I do.

I am particularly grateful to my friend and editor, Bert Ghezzi, for encouraging me to write and for his helpful guidance through this book. I am also grateful for the collaboration of the OSV team, led by Greg Erlandson, and the able editorial and marketing direction of Beth McNamara, John Christensen, Polly King, Cathy Dee, and so many more. As a Catholic publishing company, OSV has demonstrated a consistent desire to contribute to the ongoing momentum for Catholic Bible study and the New Evangelization.

Recovering
the Evangelical
Dimension
of Catholicism

Chapter 1

The Word of God and the New Evangelization

Calling Scripture "God's Handbook for Evangelizing Catholics" points to the power of God's word for forming his people as a community of witnesses. The work of evangelization is rooted in the apostolic church and is the ongoing mission of the church through the ages. Today, the people of God are challenged by the Holy Spirit to take up the call anew — to engage in a New Evangelization for the sake of God's mission in the world. "Evangelizing Catholics" emphasizes the fact that Catholics must be evangelizers if we are to be true to our identity, but the term also stresses the reality that we must first be evangelized ourselves if we are to effectively evangelize others.

The heart of this book is a demonstration of the intimate connection between the word of God and the New Evangelization. As we learn to listen to the word of God, we learn how to witness to the word of God. The more we receive that divine word into our hearts, the more our lives will reflect that word to the world. This is the way it has always been in the church, and this is the challenge offered to all Catholic Christians today in the church's third millennium.

In the latter decades of the twentieth century, the life of the church was marked by a biblical renewal. This return to Scripture, so compellingly encouraged by the Second Vatican Council, has had a striking influence on the worldwide community of faith. Through the revised lectionary with its wide selection of Scripture readings and the encouragement of biblical preaching, through the deepening of biblical theology, and through Bible courses, conferences, and parish and personal Bible studies, the people of God have begun to more clearly understand the Bible as the book of the church.

At the same time, the church began to more visibly reflect its evangelical dimensions. The Council called the church both to renew itself and to reach beyond its own community, to communicate the faith anew to the modern world. The *Dogmatic Constitution on Divine Revelation* begins with a striking call to both listen to and witness to the word of God. The church, it affirms, "hearing the word of God with reverence and proclaiming it confidently," desires to hand on God's revelation "so that by hearing the message of salvation the whole world may believe; by believing, it may hope, and by hoping, it may love."[1] The *Dogmatic Constitution on the Church* lays out the church's task to proclaim the gospel, "to unfold more fully to the faithful of the church and to the whole world its own inner nature and universal mission."[2] The *Decree on the Church's Missionary Activity* linked the church's mission with the mission of God and the life of the Trinity: "The pilgrim church is missionary by her very nature, since it is from the mission of the Son and the mission of the Holy Spirit that she draws her origin, in accordance with the decree of God the Father."[3] Taking up its evangelizing mission anew, the church must shine the light of the gospel of Jesus Christ to all.

**As we learn to listen to the word of God,
we learn how to witness to the word of God.**

In the twenty-first century, this momentum of renewal has taken concrete form in two specific tasks of the church. Pope Benedict set forth the path for the years ahead: "Our own time, then, must be increasingly marked by a new hearing of God's word and a new evangelization."[4] In describing the relationship between hearing God's word and witnessing God's word, Pope Benedict stated that "recovering the centrality of the divine word in the Christian

---

1   *Dei Verbum*, 1.
2   *Lumen Gentium*, 1.
3   *Ad Gentes*, 2.
4   Pope Benedict XVI, *Verbum Domini*, 122.

life" leads us "vigorously to embark upon the new evangelization." He highlighted the example of Paul, the great evangelizer, "who changed the course of his life after hearing the voice of the Lord" (cf. Acts 9:1–30). "In our day too," he said, "the Holy Spirit constantly calls convinced and persuasive hearers and preachers of the word of the Lord."

Pope Francis continues to make the New Evangelization the priority for the church in our times.

This interrelationship between the word of God heard in Scripture and the word of God witnessed in the New Evangelization is also demonstrated in the two consecutive synods of bishops in Rome. The first, dedicated to "The Word of God in the Life and Mission of the Church" (2008), was followed by the second, "The New Evangelization for the Transmission of the Christian Faith" (2012). The discussions and documents arising from these two international synods point out how a new hearing of God's word leads to a new witness to God's word in evangelization.

Pope Francis continues to make the New Evangelization the priority for the church in our times. His teachings present Christianity in an invitational way and call on the church to come out of itself to evangelize. "When the church does not come out of itself to evangelize", he says, "it becomes self-referential and then gets sick." He urges the church to be outward-looking, to evangelize with apostolic zeal, to be a community of "missionary disciples," living the gospel with joy and hope for the sake of the world. Yet, like his predecessors, he insists that evangelization must be rooted in God's word: "All evangelization is based on [the word of God], listened to, meditated upon, lived, celebrated, and witnessed to. The sacred Scriptures are the very source of evangelization. Consequently, we need to be constantly trained in hearing the word. The Church does not evangelize unless she constantly lets herself be evangelized." [5]

In this book, I want to continue to show more personally and practically how the word of God in Scripture and the New

---

5   Pope Francis, *Evangelii Gaudium*, 174.

Evangelization are related, how they interact with one another, and how each is necessary for the other. I want to demonstrate how love for the word of God leads to a new zeal for evangelization. Today, the Holy Spirit through the voice of God's church is calling Catholic Christians to be soaked in Scripture so that we can be heralds of the gospel of Jesus Christ to the world.

Hearing God's Word Anew through Lectio Divina

Catholics listen to God's word in Scripture in many different ways: first of all, in the church's liturgy, but also through parish programs of faith formation, Bible study, and personal, reflective reading. In all these contexts, we are invited to listen to the words of Scripture as the living word of God. Listening to the words of the Bible becomes truly renewing and transformative when we expect to encounter God and to be changed.

This way of listening to Scripture is called by its ancient name: lectio divina. This practice, as understood in the church's earliest centuries, is not so much a method of reading Scripture as it is a way of approaching the sacred text. It is not essentially a series of steps to follow, but approaching Scripture with the firm belief that God is revealed there.

Listening to the words of the Bible becomes truly renewing and transformative when we expect to encounter God and to be changed.

Through my own research into this ancient tradition, I've tried to synthesize the art of lectio divina into a few brief points. If you are hearing Scripture in these ways, then you are practicing the sacred art of lectio divina:[6]

- *Lectio divina is a personal encounter with God through Scripture.* The text itself is a gateway to God. Through the inspired Scripture, we meet the God who loves us and desires our response.

---

6   See Stephen J. Binz, *Conversing with God in Scripture: A Contemporary Approach to Lectio Divina* (Ijamsville, MD: The Word Among Us Press, 2008).

- *Lectio divina establishes a dialogue between the reader of Scripture and God.* We listen to God through the text and then respond to God in heartfelt prayer. The heart of lectio divina is this gentle conversation with God.

- *Lectio divina leads to the understanding that Jesus Christ is the heart of the Scriptures.* Every word of the Bible bears witness to the living Word who is Christ. So lectio divina is not so much a matter of interpreting a book as it is of seeking Christ in the word of God.

- *Lectio divina creates a heart-to-heart intimacy with God in Jesus Christ.* In the Bible, the heart is a person's innermost core, the source of our deepest desires and aspirations. In lectio divina we respond to God's word with the whole heart and thereby grow in a relationship with God at the deepest level of intimacy.

- *Lectio divina is a way of prayerfully reading Scripture that not only informs us but transforms us.* This divine encounter leads not just to more information and advice from the words of the Bible, but to a deeply rooted transformation of life. The deepest work of Scripture is leading us to personal growth in Christ and fuller discipleship.

This is essentially the way that most Christians have read Scripture through the ages. It is the way of the ancient church, of the fathers and mothers of the desert and monasteries, the spiritual masters, and the saints through the ages.

The return to this ancient way of reading the Bible today helps us to understand Scripture in a way that is truly personal. It helps us avoid the reductionistic reading that is characteristic of our modern age: a reading that seeks only factual information. Lectio divina teaches us to listen to the *sacra pagina*, the sacred text, in the way that God's people have heard God's word for thousands of years.

In his masterful apostolic exhortation *Verbum Domini*, Pope Benedict said this:

"I express my heartfelt hope for the flowering of a new season of greater love for sacred Scripture on the part of every member of the People of God, so that their prayerful and faith-filled reading of the Bible will, with time, deepen their personal relationship with Jesus."[7]

This hope corresponds to Pope Benedict's teachings on lectio divina. He urges God's people to cultivate not just greater understanding of the Bible, but "greater love for sacred Scripture." This love is nurtured not just through a greater intellectual study of the text, but through "prayerful and faith-filled reading." By planting, watering, and caring for the seeds of God's word in this way, we will harvest the fruit of a "personal relationship with Jesus."

The practice of lectio divina can give new intensity to Bible study, new power to preaching and catechesis, and new vigor for evangelization.

Pope Francis describes lectio divina as "listening to what the Lord wishes to tell us in his word and of letting ourselves be transformed by the Spirit."[8] He insists that lectio divina is not something separate from study of the biblical text. Rather, one's listening to Scripture "should begin with that study and then go on to discern how that same message speaks to his own life." If study is not part of lectio divina, Pope Francis adds, "we can easily make the text say what we think is convenient, useful for confirming us in our previous decisions, suited to our own patterns of thought."

This is the kind of renewed listening to God's word that can lead to the biblical renaissance that is so eagerly anticipated in the church today. This understanding of biblical reading can truly move people from initial interest to genuine discipleship. The practice of lectio divina can give new intensity to Bible study, new power to preaching and catechesis, and new vigor for evangelization. When people learn to experience Scripture with their minds,

---

7   Pope Benedict XVI, *Verbum Domini*, 72.
8   Pope Francis, *Evangelii Gaudium*, 152.

hearts, senses, emotions, and hopes engaged, they can truly encounter the Word made flesh through the written word of God.

Witnessing to God's Word through the New Evangelization

The mission of the church is the witness of the word of God to the world. So the more God's people engage in prayerful and faith-filled reading of the Bible and thereby deepen their relationship with Jesus Christ, the more they are able to participate in the church's mission of evangelization. The more we become biblical Catholics, the more we will become evangelizing Catholics.

For the church to be faithful to the gospel, it must always be offering God's gift of salvation to the world. The church is missionary and evangelical by its very nature. As disciples of Jesus and members of his church, we must proclaim the good news of Jesus with our lives. The gospel is not an exclusive gift for those who have received it; it is a gift to be shared. But this vocation to evangelize cannot be delegated to others. In baptism, we take on the lifelong mission of bringing the gospel to others. And, as St. Cyril of Jerusalem said in the fourth century, we become "bearers of Christ" when we partake of his body and blood, and so we witness to him wherever we go.

Pope Paul VI, in the years following Vatican II, urged the church to evangelize through his apostolic exhortation *Evangelization in the Modern World.* He indicates how the witness of Christians stirs up questions in the hearts of those who see how they live:

> Above all the gospel must be proclaimed by witness. Take a Christian or a handful of Christians who, in the midst of their own community, show their capacity for understanding and acceptance, their sharing of life and destiny with other people, their solidarity with the efforts of all for whatever is noble and good. Let us suppose that, in addition, they radiate in an altogether simple and unaffected way their faith in values that go beyond current values, and their hope in something that is not seen and that one would not dare to imagine. Through this wordless witness these Christians stir

up irresistible questions in the hearts of those who see how
they live: Why are they like this? Why do they live in this
way? What or who is it that inspires them? Why are they in
our midst? Such a witness is already a silent proclamation of
the good news and a very powerful and effective one. Here
we have an initial act of evangelization.

Stirring up these questions prepares the soil for the seed of
God's word. This initial act of evangelization, however, is insuffi-
cient and must be followed by a verbal response to these questions.
Focusing on the heart of genuine witness, Pope Paul VI went on
to say:

> The Good News proclaimed by the witness of life sooner or
> later has to be proclaimed by the word of life. There is no true
> evangelization if the name, the teaching, the life, the prom-
> ises, the kingdom, and the mystery of Jesus of Nazareth, the
> Son of God are not proclaimed.[9]

The gospel offers us a whole new way of seeing the world, a
fuller vision of our own lives and the lives of one another. While
we can never impose this good news of God's love in Jesus Christ,
we are called to bring it to others and let them know of the beauty
of life in Christ. We must resist the tendency to treat our Catholic
convictions as a private matter. Our faith is not a costume that we
put on for particular occasions. Only when faith permeates every
aspect of our lives can we truly open the hearts of others to the
transforming power of the gospel.

**The gospel offers us a whole new way of seeing the world,
a fuller vision of our own lives and the lives of one another.**

Cardinal Donald Wuerl tells the story of a young woman
whom he had greeted many times over the years after Mass at his
cathedral. Having assumed she was a Catholic, he was surprised
to see her in the RCIA. When he asked her what took her so long
to decide to enter the church, she replied very simply, "No one

---

9   Pope Paul VI, *Evangelii Nuntiandi*, 21–22.

ever asked me." Cardinal Wuerl explains that the New Evangelization must stir up within us a willingness and desire to share the faith. This can take the form of an invitation to those like this woman, to those who have drifted away from the practice of the faith, or to those who are searching to satisfy the longings of their hearts. "We are called," he says, "not just to announce but to adapt our approach so as to attract and to urge an entire generation to find again the uncomplicated, genuine, and tangible treasure of friendship with Jesus."[10]

Obstructions to Hearing and Witnessing God's Word Today

The challenges of hearing the word of God in lectio divina and witnessing the word of God in the New Evangelization are essentially the same task the church has taken on in every age. The word of God is always the same. We proclaim the same truth taught and lived by Jesus. Yet, the work of both listening and witnessing is particularly difficult in our day because of the obstructions presented by our cultural setting. Here are a few of the cultural obstacles to God's word being implanted in the minds and hearts of individuals and society today.

This increasing secularization of culture has resulted in a declining capacity for people to listen and understand the words of the gospel as a true and life-giving message.

The first is secularism. In a general sense, secularism is the separation of government and social institutions from religion. In some ways secularism can be healthy for both religion and society, such as the legal separation of church and state and the insistence on the essentially lay character of politics. However, a dangerous secularism refers to a culture that has crossed the line from neutrality to outright hostility toward religion and that denies the divine truths upon which traditional society is based.

---

10   Cardinal Donald Wuerl, *New Evangelization: Passing on the Catholic Faith Today* (Huntington, IN: Our Sunday Visitor, 2013), p. 83.

Revealed truths in this kind of secular culture are considered illegitimate since they cannot be supported by measurable, scientific testing. This results in the separation of transcendent truth and values from social and political life. Many who favor this increasing secularization in society see it as a liberation from the ways of the past and the way to a more tolerant culture. Those who hold to traditional religion, however, see this kind of secularization as a dangerous rejection of the transcendent truths that uplift culture and hold it together.

Although the existence of God is sometimes denied in today's culture, more often secularization fosters a mentality in which God is simply left out of human consciousness and affairs. Revealed truth has become something that today's believers are encouraged to experience within their own private lives but to leave out of the public domain. The traditional days of religious festivals, fasts, and days of prayer and thanksgiving are increasingly terminated or made a matter of personal preference. Secularism holds that human life should be guided exclusively by considerations derived from present and practical need, and that anything that is above or beyond the present life is not a matter for consideration in public life. Ultimate human purpose and destiny are beyond the purview of the secular culture. This increasing secularization of culture has resulted in a declining capacity for people to listen and understand the words of the gospel as a true and life-giving message.

The second obstacle to God's word today is rationalism. This system of thought holds that human reason is the sole arbiter and the final test of all truth. In this sense, reason is self-sufficient and does not need the help of divine revelation to know all that is necessary for human well-being. Absolute rationalism holds itself in opposition to Christian faith and considers it a hindrance to the possibilities of human perfection. All supernatural and miraculous aspects of the Bible are considered poetic fancies.

Catholic thought has always defended the importance of human reason in seeking truth. Pope John Paul II stated, "Faith and reason are like two wings on which the human spirit rises to the contemplation of truth."[11] Faith and reason both seek evidence:

---

11   Pope John Paul II, *Fides et Ratio*, preface.

faith refers to belief based on the indirect evidence of divine revelation, whereas reason leads to belief based on logic and direct observation. There can be no conflict between faith and reason since God is the source and giver of both. For this reason, Catholicism has a rich tradition of scientific inquiry and seeks to guide the work of science with the light of divine truth. Faith without reason leads to superstition, while reason without faith cannot know the highest forms of truth, which is God's revelation. But the supernatural gift of faith permits us to experience God in ways that reason alone cannot. Faith brings human reason to its highest fulfillment by providing the added light of divine revelation.

We cannot witness to God's word unless we know that it is not subject to changeable opinion or personal whim.

A third obstruction to hearing and witnessing God's word is relativism. This philosophical position holds that there is no absolute truth or value. All ideas have only relative, subjective value according to personal differences in perception and opinion. This skeptical position denies the capacity of the human mind and reason to arrive at genuine truth and asserts that all we can attain is personal and cultural beliefs. Taken to its extreme, each individual is faced with his own truth, different from the truth of others.

In today's culture of relativism, the truths of faith and religion tend to be viewed as merely personal opinions. This is essentially a denial of God, since God is absolute truth. Pope Benedict stated that we are moving toward "a dictatorship of relativism that does not recognize anything as certain and which has as its highest goal one's own ego and one's own desires." Christian faith, however, rests in the certainty of God's revealing word. It is a faith that does not follow the waves of trends and the latest novelties. "A mature faith is deeply rooted in friendship with Jesus Christ, a friendship that opens us up to all that is good and gives us the knowledge to judge true from false, and deceit from truth."[12] We cannot truly hear God's word unless we trust that it expresses divine truth, and

---

12   Mass "Pro Eligendo Romano Pontifice," homily of Cardinal Joseph Ratzinger.

we cannot witness to God's word unless we know that it is not subject to changeable opinion or personal whim.

A fourth obstacle today is individualism. In Western culture today, the freedom of individuals to maximize their own self-interest and pursue their own private ends is restricted only by the rights of other individuals to do the same. We have lost the traditional sense of the common good. Human life no longer has a purpose that is commonly agreed upon or a conception of the good toward which human life is to aim. We no longer know what it means to strive toward the communal cultivation of virtues based on a communal understanding of what human nature ought to be. So, individuals are free to choose their own personal values and to live life in a way that leads to their own satisfaction.

Such individualism creates obstacles for the hearing and witnessing to God's word, to revelation from a higher source of authority than one's self about the meaning and goal of human life. Unfortunately, even many Christians today see the church only as a place where they can get their private spiritual needs met. This pursuit of religious self-interest concerns itself simply with maintaining a personal relationship with Jesus and the pursuit of individual salvation.

The foundational principle of hearing God's word and witnessing to God's word is that God can be known and wants to be known.

The Scriptures and Catholic teaching are entirely incompatible with today's individualism. Judeo-Christian faith, from its very beginning, existed as a corporate reality. The two dominant images of the church in the Bible — the people of God and the body of Christ — present Christianity as a community filled with the presence of the risen Lord and animated by the Holy Spirit. Nobody could be Christian as an isolated individual, but only together with the body, in communion as the church. We pray together for the coming of God's kingdom, and we do the work of justice and love as a tangible expression that the reign of God is upon us.

And the fifth cultural obstacle to God's word being implanted in the minds of hearts of individuals and society today is consumerism. The focal point of cities is no longer the cathedral spire topped with the cross, but the skyscraper filled with business offices topped with the corporate logo of its owner. Our attention has been diverted from the carvings on the portals and the stained glass of the arches to the flashy ads and marketing campaigns of competing conglomerates. Rampant consumerism has perverted human desires by redirecting them from their natural end in God to an artificial objective in material objects and temporary pleasures. Yet, people eventually become discontent with our civilization of gadgets and entertainment, and they seek some overarching meaning in life. This restless discontent and hunger for faith often open space in the human heart for the lasting nourishment of the gospel.

Global capitalism has replaced the Roman Empire as the context in which the word of God must be proclaimed. In this environment, the ancient call to evangelize becomes distorted. Churches who want to increase their share of the market must ask themselves what will attract customers and meet their needs. What is called evangelization looks more like church marketing. In a buyer's market of church shoppers, offering multiple social choices and options for self-improvement becomes the first goal while less marketable aspects of Christian faith are removed.

Yet, in spite of all the obstacles of today's culture — secularism, rationalism, relativism, individualism, and consumerism — we can still profess with conviction that the gospel of Jesus Christ continues to be the answer to the truest needs and the deepest longings of the human heart. The challenge that faces the church today is how to offer the authentic good news of God's reign to a world staggering under the weight of so many unanswered questions and unfulfilled longings.

The foundational principle of hearing God's word and witnessing to God's word is that God can be known and wants to be known. The first communication of God to humanity is found within humanity itself, in our very existence. In fact, the desire for God is written in the human heart. The fact that every person desires truth and that every human being desires the ultimate experience of life is a foundational principle for any human com-munity. We are created by God and for God, and God never ceases to draw us to himself. Only in God will we find the truth and hap-piness we never stop searching for.

Human nature shares a common ground and thus is fertile soil for the seed of God's word. To be human is to seek God, the fullness of being, the ultimate truth. This search for the divine is common to every human person. Only the obstructions of our culture cloud our perceptions and obscure the evidence. But to-gether human beings can discern a common ground where the discussion about God can begin, a discussion that begins with what people have already experienced, the natural yearning for transcendent truth and goodness toward which all people are by nature inclined. Because of this common ground, we are confi-dent in the possibility of speaking about God with all people and, therefore, dialoguing with all people, including people of other religions, those engaged in philosophy and science, as well as with unbelievers and atheists.

Many people today might claim to be believers, to be bap-tized as Christians, yet they live like unbelievers, as practical athe-ists. As baptized but not evangelized, they live within all the ob-stacles of our culture, pursuing the four pernicious Ps of power, possessions, pleasure, and prestige. In practice, they ignore the four gracious Gs of God, goodness, grace, and generosity. Trying to fill the human longing for God with the temporal and materials things of this world is ultimately a fruitless effort.

We cannot protect our faith by yielding to secularization and retreating to some obscure corner of society.

God's word, the divine communication to which all people are called to listen and witness, is the foundation of human life. It contains our truest purpose and our ultimate goal. It is, in the full-est sense of the term, objective truth. Responding to God's word in faith is not just a personal choice among the many options that life offers us. The response of faith is our response to what God intends for us. Yet the influence of so many obstructions within today's culture bans from public discussion any claim to universal truth or recognition of universal moral principles. When believers proclaim fidelity to God's revelation, they are shunned as sectarian. The unrelenting secularist forces in society have convinced people that faith is not a response to what God desires for all people, but rather a personal act of sentimentalism.

Our initial reaction to the many obstacles to faith in today's culture might be confusion, fear, and withdrawal. These obstructions can cause us to question our identity and the very foundations of our faith. The fact that God is increasingly being driven out of our society makes it seem that God's revelation in Scripture is locked into an ever more remote past. Yet, we cannot retreat; we must be faithful to the priceless gift we have received. Of course, faith must always be thought out afresh and lived in new ways. We've got to learn to express God's unchanging truth in ways that it can be heard within our culture today. We've got to live and bear witness to our faith in ways that are seen as authentic by people of our times. We cannot protect our faith by yielding to secularization and retreating to some obscure corner of society. It is only by deepening God's word within us and living that word in its fullness that we can be faithful to our call and offer the gift of faith to the world today.

Becoming Evangelical Catholics

Way back in 1992, Cardinal Avery Dulles, in a talk at Fordham University, said, "Today we seem to be witnessing the birth of a new Catholicism that, without loss of its institutional, sacramental, and social dimensions, is authentically evangelical." For the remainder of his life, until his death in 2008, he spoke about the evangelical dimensions of Catholicism in our day.[13] He and so many other Catholic scholars and leaders in recent years have convinced us that being evangelical does not necessarily mean being Protestant. It means being faithful to the best and truest within the Catholic tradition.

---

13   See Avery Cardinal Dulles, S.J., *Evangelization for the Third Millennium* (New York: Paulist Press, 2009).

Evangelical movements within Christianity generally have several characteristics in common. First, they stress the central importance of Jesus Christ and cultivating a personal and genuine relationship with him. Second, they emphasize the saving death and resurrection of Christ and the need for personal conversion to the gospel. And third, they highlight devotion to inspired Scripture and the importance of sharing the "*evangel,*" that is, the good news with others. Of course none of these things is in any way opposed to Catholic teaching. In fact, they express some of the preeminent characteristics of the one, holy, catholic, and apostolic faith.

Certainly the Catholic Church has been involved in evangelization throughout its long history. In recent centuries, however, Catholics have shied away from speaking about spreading the gospel and evangelization, being content to focus on tradition, priesthood, sacraments, and saints. Turned in on itself, the church was more comfortable with the instruction and pastoral care of its own members than with reaching out to new members. Evangelizing was understood as missionary activity to foreign lands, a work that was reserved primarily for certain orders and missionary societies.

Evangelization is a lifelong process by which people's lifestyle, way of thinking, and approach to life are permeated and transformed by the gospel.

Yet, in recent decades, the Catholic Church has been imbued with a new evangelical spirit. We can see a clear line of teaching on the centrality of evangelization in the Catholic Church from the documents of Vatican II, to Pope Paul VI's *Evangelii Nuntiandi* ("On Evangelization in the Modern World"), to the exhortations in Pope John Paul II's *Redemptoris Missio* ("The Mission of the Redeemer"), to the apostolic exhortation *Evangelii Gaudium* ("The Joy of the Gospel") of Pope Francis. They demonstrate that the church must be seen as a community of disciples in mission to the world. The call to the New Evangelization by Pope John Paul, an evangelization new in its fervor, methods, and expressions, its practical implementations by Pope Benedict XVI, and the personal commitment and witness of Pope Francis continue to accelerate the church's drive into an evangelical future. Bible studies, catechetical materials, youth and young adult ministry programs, retreats, conferences, and new media initiatives witness to an increasing evangelical zeal within the church.

Evangelical Catholics are those whose lives have been radically converted to Jesus Christ, who are joyful disciples, and who are dedicated to proclaiming the gospel in word and deed. These renewed Catholics read Scripture daily, regularly celebrate the sacraments, and seek to infuse their lives with holiness and mission. These Catholics evangelize because they believe that their faith is true, that it is revealed by God, and that God wants all people to come to a knowledge of this saving truth. The New Evangelization, then, is all about knowing the faith, having confidence in it, and sharing it with others. Every believer has a responsibility to try to share this good news, never trying to compel people to believe, but always seeking to find ways to offer the gospel of salvation in an attractive and evocative way.

A Catholic form of evangelization is never complete with an initial proclamation of the gospel to individuals. Evangelization is a lifelong process by which people's lifestyle, way of thinking, and approach to life are permeated and transformed by the gospel. Parents are the first evangelizers of their children, and homes are the primary places where spouses and family members evangelize one another. And those who have been genuinely evangelized find their home in the church as the place in which their friendship with Jesus Christ can be fully lived out.

But Catholic evangelization does not just lead people to Jesus and his church; it continually seeks to renew the church itself. The New Evangelization knows that the church itself is in continual need of being evangelized as it becomes an increasingly attractive dwelling for the Holy Spirit and witness to the risen Lord. Many baptized Catholics are in need of evangelization. Some who have received early instructions in the faith have never heard the gospel proclaimed as the good news that transforms lives. Many who know the teachings of the church have never truly encountered the living Christ. Inactive and marginal Catholics must encounter the gospel in a fresh way. Through Scripture reading, biblical preaching, and Bible study, these Catholics can energize their commitment and allow God's Spirit to revitalize their friendship with the Lord. The church will attract new members to the degree that it is a community of joyful disciples and committed witnesses, united in mind and heart as the body of Christ in the world.

In a nutshell, to evangelize is to know Christ, to make him known, and to transform individuals and society by the reality of that proclamation.

Catholic evangelization is not high-pressure proselytism. The purpose of evangelization is not to convince people to change denominations. The lack of unity among Christians damages the church's witness, and all evangelizers must promote the unity of Christians according to the will of the Lord. Every step along the path of ecumenism is a contribution to the evangelization of the non-Christian world. Evangelization must always be the loving offer of a gift, fully respecting the freedom and dignity of the other person. The gospel enters into the heart of another by its own power and never from any coercion or pressure on the part of the one presenting the good news. We bear witness to Christ in word and deed by reflecting his image, which becomes real in us through grace and the work of the Holy Spirit.

Finally, Catholic evangelization is directed to whole cultures. Societies must continually be purified, elevated, and enriched by the witness of faith. In the church's early centuries, it infiltrated the culture of Greco-Roman antiquity and gave rise to a wondrous flourishing of art, music, philosophy, and literature. The church must continually seek ways of proposing the gospel that are effective in each culture. To evangelize a culture means to cleanse it of contaminants and transform it in light of the good news of Christ. Working for the common good, action on behalf of justice, and participation in the transformation of society are essential aspects of witnessing to the gospel. Christ ennobles and refines human cultures, and his church must seek to create cultures that instill and reflect the truths and values of God's reign. If people were to follow the teachings and example of Jesus, we would establish an image of God's kingdom, a culture of solidarity and peace, a civilization of love.

Evangelization, then, is an enormous reality encompassing all that the church was founded to be. In a nutshell, to evangelize is to know Christ, to make him known, and to transform individuals and society by the reality of that proclamation. It begins with individuals who understand what it means to joyfully and faithfully follow Jesus, accepting his teaching, desiring to live as he did, embracing his cross, and living under God's reign. This transformation of life leads to a burning desire to invite others to encounter Jesus and the good news he brings to the world. This is the heart of the evangelizing mission to which the whole church is called.

For Reflection or Discussion

1. What do the words "Evangelizing Catholics" mean to you?

2. Why is there an essential connection between the word of God and the New Evangelization?

3. Pope Francis said, "When the church does not come out of itself to evangelize, it becomes self-referential and then gets sick." Why does excessive inward looking rather than outward looking lead to sickness within the church?

4. In what ways is lectio divina different from the ways that some Catholics read Scripture?

5. Why must we become biblical Catholics in order to be evangelizing Catholics?

6. Which of the obstacles to hearing and witnessing God's word seem most obstructive today? In what ways is your experience of the gospel affected by this cultural obstacle?

7. Why is the Catholic Church becoming increasingly evangelical in character? What are some of the unique characteristics of Catholic evangelization?

Chapter 2

Evangelizing Moments in Catholic History

Throughout the two-thousand-year history of the church, every major period of renewed evangelization has been the result of a return to the centrality of sacred Scripture. Whether we look at the apostolic age and the vigorous growth of the church in its earliest centuries, or the monastic movement in its various forms, or the mendicant renewal of the church in the Middle Ages, or the age of the Counter-Reformation, we can see that these periods and movements of reform have sprung from a revitalization of the church through Scripture. In each age, a renewed reading of God's written word has produced a new kindling of the Holy Spirit's fire and reawakened witness.

Looking at the individual lives of the saints, we see that their immersion in Scripture directed their lives to witness.

I believe that the lives of the saints through the ages manifest this dynamic most obviously. Truly the saints are the best interpreters of the Bible. As they incarnate the word of God in their own lives, they make it more captivating than ever. And as we see the effects of the word of God in their lives, their example speaks powerfully to us, inspiring us to be better disciples of Jesus and witnesses of the gospel to others.

Looking at the individual lives of the saints, we see that their immersion in Scripture directed their lives to witness. Their lectio divina led them to evangelization. For this reason, the saints can be great models for us as we take up the two great tasks of the church in our age: the renewed listening to the word of God, which is the tradition of lectio divina, and the renewed witness to the word of God, which is the New Evangelization. As we look to their example, we can learn to listen to the word like the saints and to witness to the word like the saints.

So I will highlight six saints who represent different periods of the church's life through the ages. I will indicate how their lives were absorbed in the deteriorating environment in which the church found itself at the time and how their listening to Scripture brought renewal to the church and a new period of evangelization.

St. Paul of Tarsus

Paul was certainly a man of the Scriptures. As a studious Jew, he had learned the Torah and the prophets at the feet of Rabbi Gamaliel in Jerusalem. As a scholar of the Hebrew Scriptures, he studied the word of God, and he chanted the inspired text in the synagogue and temple. Later, in Jerusalem, he began to violently persecute the church and its members because of his zealous dedication to the God of Israel.

Then, while he was on his way to Damascus to round up people who belonged to the new Way of Jesus so that they could be sent to Jerusalem for punishment, he experienced a light from heaven and a revelation of the Risen Jesus. We know the rest of the story of Paul's life-changing conversion and how he became the church's greatest missionary.

> **Paul's synthesis of the Christian gospel showed the early followers how to live in the midst of a pagan and often hostile Roman Empire.**

What we don't know is what happened between his conversion and his missionary journeys. Very briefly, Paul tells us at the beginning of his letter to the Galatians: "When God was pleased to reveal his Son to me, so that I might proclaim him among the Gentiles, I did not confer with any human being, nor did I go up to Jerusalem to those who were already apostles before me, but I went away at once into Arabia" (Gal 1:16–17). Rather than immediately going to discuss this revelation with Peter and the other apostles in

Jerusalem, as we would expect, he went into a deserted region, to the East of the Dead Sea. It was three years before he returned and went up to Jerusalem, where he stayed for two weeks.

What did Paul do in Arabia during that time? Why did he not immediately go to Jerusalem, where the new Way of Jesus had begun and from where his gospel was being proclaimed? Why did he not begin evangelizing right away? Why spend three years in relative solitude? It seems obvious to me that Paul was reading the Scriptures again in the light of the risen Lord. He was studying the ancient Hebrew texts in light of the new revelation God had given to him. Then, after his lectio divina, his transformative listening to Scripture, he was able to confirm his understanding with the apostles in Jerusalem and then launch his career as the greatest evangelizer the world has ever known.

Throughout Paul's missionary life, as we see in Acts and in his letters, Paul explained how Jesus the Messiah is the completion of the Scriptures of Israel, how the law and the prophets are fulfilled in him. Paul's speeches are filled with quotes and references from the Old Testament as he proclaims the good news of Jesus Christ. So, we see that his study of Scripture leads him to witness; his lectio divina leads to evangelization.

Paul's synthesis of the Christian gospel showed the early followers how to live in the midst of a pagan and often hostile Roman Empire. Within that difficult context, Christians learned to live as an alternative community, shaped by the alternative narrative of the new covenant. And the teaching ministry of the church had as its purpose to empower a distinct people shaped by God's word.

This alternative community was an attractive sign of the kingdom of God in the midst of the Roman Empire. In a world that called the emperor their lord and savior, the Christian community proclaimed that Jesus is the true Lord of all and the Savior of the whole world. The teachings and writings of Paul proclaimed the gospel and were designed to lead people to faith, to a life of deep friendship and community with Jesus, to a life "in Christ."

The new church was an engaging counter-sign. It broke down barriers between rich and poor, free and slave, woman and man, Jew and Gentile. The gospel of love was lived out for the poor, orphans, widows, travelers, slaves, the sick, and the prisoners. The lives of Christians stood out against the decadent, materialistic, unfaithful lives within the Roman Empire. Christians were known for their simple lifestyles, fidelity in marriage, generosity with their possessions, their charity toward others, and even their love for enemies.

Believers were disciples and witnesses, living lives that were shaped by the teachings of Jesus and that bore witness to him. The early church did not allow itself to be pushed into a private religion, hidden in some obscure corner of Roman society. Its witness was publicly subversive. The church refused to conform to the norms of the Empire, and it lived the values of the gospel instead. It saw itself as the vanguard of a new humanity, a community called to bear witness to the kingdom of God in the midst of the world.

And these Christian communities grew like wildfire. Nowhere else in the Roman world did men and women gather and worship together, nowhere else did slaves and masters call one another brothers and sisters, nowhere else did Jews and Gentiles gather at the same table, nowhere else did rich and poor share their goods and recognize that they were all redeemed sinners. The gospel of the Jewish Messiah, the risen Lord, changed hearts and transformed lives. And everyone wanted to be a part of it — everyone, of course, except those who had too many possessions and too much power to lose. The church was an evangelizing community, empowered by the Holy Spirit to let the word of God shine out with their lives.

The early decades of the church saw the first age of the martyrs. Both Paul and Peter, and many other Christians, witnessed to the faith in the most courageous way, by dying in the name of Christ. They evangelized through the complete witness of martyrdom, and their witness was followed by many other periods of martyrdom, which has led to the new age of martyrdom that we see in many parts of the world today.

St. Benedict of Nursia

At the beginning of the sixth century, the Roman Empire had collapsed and civilization was in ruin. The invasions of new peoples and the erosion of morality created a terrible time. In writing about

St. Benedict, Pope Gregory the Great called him a "luminous star" pointing the way out of "the black night of history."

Benedict was born in a small village near Rome and was educated in the city. But he left his studies to live in the solitude of the mountainous area of Subiaco. He lived alone as a hermit for three years in a cave that is today called the Sacro Speco (the Holy Grotto). Those years were a period of maturing, overcoming temptations, and commitment to Christ. He listened to God's word, prayed in response to God's word, and in contemplation he allowed God to form him into the image of Christ.

In writing about St. Benedict, Pope Gregory the Great called him a "luminous star" pointing the way out of "the black night of history."

Only after this contemplative period of listening to Scripture did he decide to establish his first monastery in the valley near Subiaco. This foundation was followed by twelve daughter monasteries and the beginning of his writing his famous Rule. He then left Subiaco for Cassino, where he converted the population from paganism and built the famous Montecassino Monastery. It was there that he died in 547, after completing the final version of the Benedictine Rule, which would become the standard guideline for Western monasticism

The contrast between Subiaco, which is a remote and hidden monastery, and Montecassino, which was built on a mountain plateau, dominating the surrounding plain and seen from afar, seems to express the double purpose of monasticism. A monastery is a place where its members are hidden and cultivate an intimacy with God, and a monastery is also a public witness to Christ and his church, giving visibility to the faith and proclaiming the gospel to all.

It is said that the Benedictine monks brought civilization to Europe through "the cross, the book, and the plow" — which expresses the life of the monastery, built on the liturgy, lectio divina, and manual labor. Benedictine monks built monasteries where learning and ancient manuscripts were preserved for the ages, and

what we think of as the Christian culture of Europe is largely in-
debted to these monasteries. Pope Paul VI named Benedict as the
patron saint of Europe for the formation of the civilization and culture of the continent. As Europe searches for its own identity today
and seeks to create a new and lasting unity, political, economic,
and juridical instruments are important. But it is also necessary to
awaken an ethical and spiritual renewal which draws on its Christian roots, otherwise a new Europe cannot be firmly built.

**The monks sought God in sacred Scripture and then
allowed that searching to shape their entire lives
of commerce and industry.**

In the monasteries of Benedict, bells called the monks to
prayer, and the hours of the day were marked by praying Scripture.
In chanting the psalms, the monks prayed the prayers of Jesus and
prayed in union with him. In the early morning and late evening
hours, the Scriptures were prayed by candlelight. Reading from
Scripture was followed by periods of meditative silence. Soaked in
Scripture, immersion in the Bible led to an ever-deepening immersion in the life of God.

The monastery was the heart of a whole city. Beyond the
church and cloister, land was developed for livestock, mining, and
agriculture. *Ora et Labora* ("prayer and work") was the Benedictine motto. The monks sought God in sacred Scripture and then
allowed that searching to shape their entire lives of commerce and
industry. Through Scripture, they learned to be present to God in
the moment: cooking meals, shearing sheep, teaching children,
building fences, balancing account books, tending the sick. In that
way, their relationship with God was intimate and real.

Among the works of the monasteries was copying texts.
They produced illuminated manuscripts of the Bible and other
books — magnificent script illuminated with color and gold leaf.
These beautiful manuscripts helped the reader appreciate the
word of God. Today, when we read the Bible from paperbacks and
Bible apps, our challenge is to maintain the same attentiveness to
the text taught in the monasteries. We have to learn how to be-

come attentive to the presence of God who comes to us through the inspired text, the *sacra pagina*, the sacred Scriptures.

St. Benedict, through the gift of his Rule and the Benedictine family, founded a heritage that bore fruit in the passing centuries and is still bearing fruit throughout the world today. The Rule of Benedict, used in thousands of abbeys throughout the world, begins with its clarion call: Listen! "Listen carefully to the Master's instructions, and attend to them with the ear of your heart.... Let us listen well to what the Lord says."[14] He tells his followers to listen to God's voice in Scripture. Through Scripture, Benedict taught attentiveness and mindfulness, turning the mind and heart in the direction of God and keeping them there.

Yet, Benedict also taught that the word of God must be expressed in action. After listening and internalizing Scripture, it must be externalized in Christian witness. Benedict also says in the prologue of his Rule, "The Lord is waiting every day for us to respond to his holy admonitions by our deeds." So, the monk's life is a fruitful symbiosis between contemplation and action, "so that God may be glorified in all things." In this way, Benedict teaches us to listen to the word of God and witness to God's word. Contemplation and action are necessary for each other; lectio divina and evangelization go hand in hand.

It seems to me that the continuing attraction of the Benedictine way of life is its contrast to the way of life in our modern culture. The egocentric desires for possessions, power, and pleasure are obviously different from the sincere search for God. The path of listening, humility, and obedience to God's word is the way marked out by Jesus. Holiness of life, inspired by faith and acted out in love, is attractive and enticing, and so it is a form of witness and New Evangelization for our world today.

St. Francis of Assisi

Francis of Assisi began the renewal of the church at the beginning of the thirteenth century simply by seeking to live like Jesus. Witnessing to his followers more by his lifestyle than his words, he taught simplicity, care for the poor, the value of suffering, and living with

---

14   Benedict, *The Rule of Saint Benedict*, Prologue.

deep joy. He began one of the church's greatest periods of reform, showing people of the Middle Ages how to live like Jesus.

The son of a wealthy merchant in Assisi, at age twenty Francis took part in a military campaign, was taken prisoner, and became ill. After his return to Assisi, a slow process of spiritual conversion began within him, which brought him to see the emptiness of his frolicking lifestyle. Through reading the gospel he discovered Jesus, and he learned to follow him humbly, joyfully, and without limit. Literally stripping himself of his clothing and possessions, he gave all to the poor. Francis realized that his interior conversion was real, when one day he saw a leper along the road, and rather than avoiding the wretched man as in his former life, he dismounted from his horse and embraced the leper.

Francis of Assisi began the renewal of the church at the beginning of the thirteenth century simply by seeking to live like Jesus.

Another important moment in the life of Francis came as he was praying before an image of Christ on the cross in Assisi's church of San Damiano. Three times Christ on the cross told him, "Go, Francis, and repair my church that is in ruins." The church that was falling into ruins symbolized the state of the church at the time. Many in the church had a superficial faith; they were baptized but not evangelized. The clergy were lax, and the love at the heart of the church had grown cold. This interior destruction of the church had brought decay to the church's unity and its mission.

Yet, there at the center of the church in ruins was the crucified Lord. And as he spoke, he called for renewal. He first called Francis to the manual labor of repairing the small church of San Damiano. So Francis became a humble worker, repairing the churches of Assisi, brick by brick. This initial expression of reform was a symbol of the much deeper renewal and evangelization that Francis would bring to Christ's church with his burning faith and enthusiastic love.

For a while, Francis lived as a hermit, until one day he was listening to the gospel and heard the discourse of Jesus to the apostles as he sent them out on mission. Then Francis began gathering followers, and he taught them to literally live the gospel, carrying no gold, silver, or copper in their traveling bag and announcing the kingdom of God. Francis had no thoughts of founding a new religious order. He taught his followers to live an active life of preaching the good news while rooted in quiet times of solitary prayer. Francis's new way of religious life was lived not in monasteries, but among the people. His followers witnessed not only with the words of Scripture and the message of the gospel, but also through a lifestyle of joyful evangelical poverty, simplicity, and charity. In fact, the first rule of life that Francis wrote for his followers was a collection of texts from the gospels.

> **Francis's new way of religious life was lived not in monasteries, but among the people.**

Francis's experience of the image of Christ on the cross at the Church of San Damiano parallels a dream recounted by Pope Innocent III. In it, the Pope saw the Basilica of St. John Lateran in Rome, the mother of all churches, collapsing. But one small and insignificant religious brother was supporting the church on his shoulders to prevent it from falling. Later, when Francis and his followers came to Rome seeking permission to begin the Franciscan order, Pope Innocent recognized Francis as the religious brother in his dream. The Pope gave Francis and his brothers a fatherly welcome and approved the foundation of their new form of apostolic life. Although Innocent III was a powerful Pope who had a great theological formation and great political influence, he was not the one who would reform Christ's church. That work would be done by the small, insignificant religious brother named Francis, in union with the Pope and in service to God's people.

Francis and his friars established themselves at the Portiuncula, a small chapel around which they lived in individual cells. This Little Portion is the sacred place for Franciscans, the heart of Franciscan spirituality. A young woman of Assisi, Clare, from a noble family, followed the way of Francis. Her sisters were the origin of the second Franciscan order, the Poor Clares. Francis formed communities in other places of Europe, and the new order grew rapidly. Since Francis visited the Holy Land, today many of the churches and shrines of those biblical sites are a special place for the Franciscan mission.

St. Francis brought a renewed experiential dimension to the study of Scripture in the church. He believed that the Bible should not merely be learned, but lived out. And, although he encouraged his followers to study Scriptures, he taught that the study of the word must always be a spiritual exercise meant to convert the heart. His biblical renewal insisted on the combination of study, prayer, and self-sacrifice so that each word of Scripture is received with humility. In this way, the religious communities rooted in St. Francis have reinvigorated the church by making this unique Franciscan integration of reflective reading and prayer of Scripture the foundation of their evangelizing mission in the world.

St. Dominic of Guzman

Dominic lived at about the same time as Francis, and they simultaneously founded mendicant communities, a new form of religious life. Although Dominic and Francis met and at one time considered combining their communities, it became clear that they had different charisms for living out their mission.

When Spain was desolated by a famine, the young Dominic gave away his money and sold his clothes, furniture, and even precious manuscripts to feed the hungry.

Dominic was born and raised in Spain, and there studied the arts and theology. He distinguished himself in his young life for both his study of sacred Scripture and his love for the poor. When Spain was desolated by a famine, the young Dominic gave away his money and sold his clothes, furniture, and even precious manuscripts to feed the hungry.

On his travels, Dominic became aware of two great challenges for the church at the beginning of the thirteenth century. One was the existence of people in northern Europe to whom the gospel had never been brought. The other was the Albigensian heresy, a distortion of Christianity that denied the incarnation, the sacraments, and the resurrection of the body, which was undermining the faith in southern France. His zeal for the mission of the church led him to desire both to evangelize those who did not yet know Jesus Christ and to re-evangelize communities who had fallen away from the faith.

Dominic often urged the brothers of his Order of Preachers to constantly study the Old and New Testaments.

For the rest of his life, a missionary fire burned in the heart of Dominic, and he devoted himself to preaching the good news. He preached especially in the cities and university towns where he could dialogue with the intellectual trends of the day and bring the light of the gospel. Many others joined him, attracted by the same aspirations, and the Order of Preachers gradually came into being. They travelled from one place to another preaching, then returning to their priory, for study, prayer, and communal life. As mendicants, without monasteries to administer, they lived simply and were available for travel, preaching, and practical witness.

Dominic wanted his followers to acquire a solid theological education, and often sent them to the universities of the time to study sacred Scripture, which he knew was an important preparation for the ministry of preaching. He established houses near the celebrated universities, wanting his followers to understand the intellectual culture of the times and desiring to attract followers from the ranks of university students.

Dominic always carried with him the gospel of Matthew and the epistles of Paul, studying them constantly, so much that he nearly had them memorized. He knew that God's kingdom would be spread through the preaching of the gospel, just as Jesus had called his own followers to do. In his letters and conversations, Dominic often urged the brothers of his Order of Preachers to constantly study the Old and New Testaments. He knew that good preaching would flow from a studious, reflective, and prayerful reading of Scripture. Thus, Dominican friars study Scripture, pray the biblical texts of the Divine Office in common, practice lectio divina, and preach from Scripture, about Scripture, and in response to Scripture.

A document called the *Nine Ways of Prayer of Saint Dominic*, written by one of his followers who knew him well, is a hallmark of Dominican spirituality. Each of these nine ways is a prayer posture used by Dominic, such as bowing, prostration, and standing with arms outstretched. These gestures are an outward expression of an interior spiritual disposition, and each of these nine ways describes Dominic praying to God with words of Scripture.

The eighth way of prayer, which is a sitting posture, describes lectio divina. Dominic, in reading and praying with Scripture, appeared to be like Moses, who went into the desert to the burning bush and then listened to God speaking to him. The document states: "When he read alone in this solitary fashion, Dominic used to venerate the book, bow to it, and kiss it. This was especially true if he was reading the gospels and when he had been reading the very words which had come from the mouth of Christ."[15] The writer says that Dominic had a prophetic way of moving from reading to prayer and from meditation to contemplation.

The ninth way of prayer is done while walking. When traveling from place to place, Dominic would go ahead of his companions, or more often linger far behind them. Walking on his own, he would give himself over to meditation and contemplation. The document states: "He would walk and pray; in his meditation he was inflamed and the fire of charity was enkindled.... The brethren thought that it was while praying in this way that the saint obtained his extensive penetration of sacred Scripture and profound understanding of the divine words, the power to preach so fervently and courageously, and that intimate acquaintance with the Holy Spirit by which he came to know the hidden things of God."[16]

Dominic took the practice of lectio divina from the monastic tradition and gave it a new form. Now it was not just the listening of the solitary monk who withdrew in silence for a personal encounter with the word of God. Dominic joined lectio divina with the friar's travel from place to place, transforming it into a practice that leads to the preaching of the good news.

_____

15   Phyllis Zagano, *The Dominican Tradition* (Collegeville: Liturgical Press, 2006), p. 12.

16   Ibid., p.12.

For Dominicans the study of Scripture is an important dimension of prayer. But study is not just an intellectual exercise. Study is lectio, being silent and opening the ear, waiting for God's word to come to the listener. Followers of Dominic know that they must first receive God's word before they can share it with others. Only after receptive listening can they respond in holy preaching and living the word through the daily witness of Christian life. Preaching is sharing with the world the experience of God's kingdom, discovered through a personal encounter with the word of life.

In the Dominican tradition, study, prayer, and contemplation of Scripture were always balanced with active witness and preaching.

The biblical model for the Dominican way of life is the early Christian community in the Acts of the Apostles. Rooted in their life of prayer and their intimate friendship with their risen Lord, the apostles traveled far and wide, from one country to another, spreading the good news throughout the world. Like the apostles, and like Dominic walking with Scripture, the Order of Preachers walks courageously with the word, fervently bringing the gospel to the searching world.

In the Dominican tradition, study, prayer, and contemplation of Scripture were always balanced with active witness and preaching. Of course preaching for the followers of Dominic does not just refer to the liturgical homily. Preaching means proclaiming the good news of Jesus, witnessing to God's kingdom in word and in action. This kind of preaching the word, as a response to the prayerful study of Scripture, is a way that all Christians can imitate St. Dominic. He reminds us that the study of sacred Scripture must always lead to a pastoral yearning. One of the most famous of the Dominicans, St. Thomas Aquinas, coined a phrase that has become a motto for the Dominican family: "*Contemplare et contemplata aliis trader,*" which means, roughly, "To contemplate and share the fruits of that contemplation with others." Followers of Dominic do not simply meditate and thank God for giving them understanding and insights into the word of God, but they take the next step and share with others in teaching and preaching the insights they have gained.

When Dominic died in Bologna, his work had already had widespread success. The Order of Preachers had spread to numerous other countries in Europe, and many followed in his way. Some of the great Dominican saints are Albert the Great, Thomas Aquinas, Catherine of Siena, Rose of Lima, and Martin De Porres. They teach us that genuine evangelizing is always born from an encounter with the word of God.

St. Ignatius of Loyola

Ignatius founded the Society of Jesus in the sixteenth century, during the Protestant Reformation. In a period of confusion and crisis for the church, he helped people focus on Scripture and experience its transforming potential. His leadership assisted the church with a great Catholic reform and instilled a new missionary spirit.

As a young soldier, Ignatius was seriously injured by a cannonball and underwent a spiritual conversion during his long recovery. He read Scripture, biblical commentaries, and the lives of the saints. By meditating on Scripture, he was gradually converted. God's grace then filled Ignatius with a desire to become like Jesus, to lead a life of self-denial, and to imitate the heroic lives of the great saints. During his period of conversion, he used to muse to himself, "What if I should do what St. Francis did and what St. Dominic did?"

The *Spiritual Exercises* forms the foundation of Ignatian spirituality, a way of experiencing God in all things and living for God's glory.

He went to Manresa, where he began praying for many hours each day, often in a nearby cave, while formulating the fundamentals of his most famous work, *The Spiritual Exercises*. He wanted to help others experience Jesus Christ through meditation and prayer with Scripture. The Exercises were originally designed for a thirty-day retreat under the guidance of a spiritual director. The retreat was designed to help people experience the presence of Jesus through Scripture, to develop a relationship with him, and to make a personal commitment to follow him. Each day consists of meditation and prayer on various Scripture passages, with the goal of understanding how the biblical passages might apply to the life of the individual. Those on retreat must observe silence, pray continually for God's grace, and become increasingly attuned to God's movements in their hearts.

The Spiritual Exercises forms the foundation of Ignatian spirituality, a way of experiencing God in all things and living for God's glory. It is always concerned with discernment — continually seeking to understand what is the right path to glorify God in one's life. This spiritual path helps people learn to move away from living for their lower desires, and shows them a way to direct their energies toward the fulfillment of their higher purpose in life.

Ignatius built upon the ancient practice of prayerfully reading Scripture and added some important dimensions and spiritual disciplines. He instructed believers to become attentive to the "movements of the soul," a type of personal examination of one's current mental, emotional, and spiritual state. This is not done to become self-focused, but rather to become aware of one's needs in order to bring them before God in the time of Scripture reading and prayer. In bringing their needs before God, believers can then listen for God's response through the word and prayer. Ignatius then instructed them to engage their imagination in reading Scripture and to place themselves within the scene, becoming a participant within the story. Creating a picture of the scene with the imagination, the readers seek to notice the details and ask themselves what they see, hear, smell, taste, and feel. As a participant in the story, the readers imagine themselves as a disciple, a person being healed, a member of the crowd being taught, or any number of roles.

The point of these exercises is to enable an encounter with Jesus himself through the biblical story — an account that is not just history, but the story of every believer. By engaging in Scripture, believers engage Jesus in their own story of life. This sacred reading of the biblical text then leads the readers to respond to what they have experienced by beginning a spiritual conversation with Jesus within the scene. That conversation, listening and responding, then continues as they learn to discern how God is leading them.

The Ignatian tradition places great emphasis on the transition from prayer to witness.

After writing *The Spiritual Exercises*, Ignatius spent seven years of study at the University of Paris. By the end of his studies, he had gathered six key companions, all of whom he met as fellow students at the university. Ignatius and his six companions then took upon themselves the solemn vows of their lifelong work and became the Society of Jesus, soon to be known to the world as the Jesuits. As the first Father General, Ignatius sent his companions as missionaries around Europe to create schools, colleges, and seminaries. The new order later fanned out beyond Europe to the Americas and Far East. The main principle of Ignatius became the Jesuit motto: *Ad maiorem Dei gloriam* ("For the greater glory of God").

St. Ignatius of Loyola, in his *Spiritual Exercises*, wrote that we are created to "praise, reverence, and serve God." Our one desire and choice should be what is most conducive to this end for which we are created. This choice to be a disciple is summarized in his Suscipe: "Take Lord, and receive all my liberty, my memory, my understanding, and my entire will, all that I have and possess. Thou hast given all to me. To Thee, O Lord, I return it. All is Thine, dispose of it wholly according to Thy will. Give me Thy love and Thy grace, for this is sufficient for me."

The Ignatian tradition places great emphasis on the transition from prayer to witness. Personal contact with the word of God must nourish the faith, hope, and love made manifest in daily choices. This is especially necessary today, when daily experience of the gospel is more difficult to find and outward signs of the mystery of God are harder to recognize. Through the disciplines and practices taught by St. Ignatius Loyola, we can move with discernment from meditative listening to Scripture to witness in daily life, from prayerful reflection to evangelization.

St. Thérèse of Lisieux

Like all of these saints, Thérèse of Lisieux lived at a time of crisis for the church. In the final decades of the nineteenth century, France experienced an extended and often bloody struggle between the Catholic royalists and the more secular republic. It was an age of rationalism, the church was under siege, and many Catholics withdrew into a kind of pietistic and devotional faith.

The key to Thérèse's wisdom was her love for Scripture, which was uncharacteristic of Catholics at the time.

The life of Thérèse seemed also to be withdrawn, spending the last years of her short life in the Carmelite monastery of Lisieux, where she died of tuberculosis at the age of twenty-four. But after her death, her autobiography became an international bestseller that evangelized millions and brought them to a deep love for Jesus. When she was canonized in 1925, she became easily the most popular saint of the twentieth century.

Along with the great Jesuit missionary Francis Xavier, Thérèse of Lisieux was named co-patron of missionaries, even though she never set foot on mission territory. As a contemplative nun, she never ceased to live the missionary impulses of the Christian vocation. Her contemplation of Scripture was always united with its evangelizing dimension, and in letters to missionaries in foreign countries, she emphasized the apostolic dimension of her contemplative life.

The key to Thérèse's wisdom was her love for Scripture, which was uncharacteristic of Catholics at the time. In the last quarter of the nineteenth century, the time in which Thérèse lived, Catholics paid all too little attention to Scripture. Books were expensive, and many pastors discouraged personal reading and interpretation. Yet, in the French edition of Thérèse's writings there are twenty-three pages listing citations of over a thousand biblical quotations. This fact alone is impressive, but even more so is the biblical imagination that pervaded Thérèse's consciousness and that nourished the love which enlarged her heart. Sister Thérèse of the Child Jesus was no biblical scholar, but she was drenched in the wisdom of the word of God that gave her a language of prayer. And for this reason, Pope John Paul II named her one of the Doctors of the Church, one of only four women to ever be given that title.

In the Carmelite tradition, Thérèse listened to Scripture read each day in the refectory and in the celebration of the Eucharist and the Divine Office. She found in the psalms the expressions that translated her own feelings, and she meditated on the biblical readings. She knew, as did Solomon, that wisdom comes from listening to the word of God with a listening heart (1 Kings 3:9). She was convinced that when she read Scripture she was in fact listening to Jesus who was speaking to her through the sacred texts. And in the line of Carmelite spirituality which teaches people to be contemplatives, Thérèse knew that this lectio divina leads to the highest form of prayer, which is silence in the loving presence of God.

In addition to the biblical readings that Thérèse heard in the course of her communal life, she showed a voracious hunger for Scripture, an appetite that fueled her passionate relationship with Jesus. Since complete Bibles were uncommon and owning one was a rare privilege, Thérèse looked for biblical quotations in other books and wherever she could find them. The only books that Thérèse had for her own use were the four gospels, which she always carried with her on her heart.

Trust and love are the key to the "Little Way," a gift that Thérèse has given to us all.

The autobiography of Thérèse, *Story of a Soul*, shows that the word of God led her from one step to another on her spiritual journey. Insights from Scripture confirmed her own spiritual intuitions. And it was especially in her discovery of her famous "Little Way" that Scripture played a fundamental role. As a young woman, Thérèse wanted deeply to become a saint. She dreamed of being a warrior like Joan of Arc or a great missionary in foreign lands. But her circumstances and her fragile health prevented her from doing any of those things. Instead, she searched the Scriptures and read the words, "Whoever is a little one, let him come to me" (Prov 9:4).

She continued to search and discovered the words of Isaiah: "As one whom a mother caresses, so will I comfort you; you shall be carried at the breasts and upon the knees they shall caress you" (Isa 66:12–13). These tender words gave her great joy, and she realized that in order to serve God, she had to remain little and become even more little.[17]

Through her "Little Way" of childlike confidence and trust in God, Thérèse describes her discovery of a passage from Paul's letter, 1 Corinthians 12–13, in which he says that we can't all be apostles, or prophets, or teachers. The church is composed of many members who differ from one another. Then she continued to read that all the gifts of heaven, even the most perfect, are absolutely nothing without love. Charity is the best way of all because it leads straight to God. She writes this about finding her place in the church:

"Considering the mystical body of the church, I had not recognized myself in any of the members described by St. Paul, or rather I desired to see myself in them all. Charity gave me the key to my vocation. I understood that if the church had a body composed of different members, the most necessary and most noble of all could not be lacking to it, and so I understood that the church had a heart and that this heart was burning with love. I understood it was love alone that made the church's members act, that if love ever became extinct, apostles would not preach the gospel and martyrs would not shed their blood. I understood that love comprised all vocations, that love was everything, that it embraced all times and places, in a word, that it was eternal. Then, in the excess of my delirious joy, I cried out: O Jesus, my Love, my vocation, at last I have found it. My vocation is love! Yes, I have found my place in the church and it is you, O my God, who have given this place; in the heart of the church, my mother, I shall be love. Thus I shall be everything, and thus my dream will be realized."[18]

---

17   *Story of a Soul*, translated by John Clark, O.C.D. (Washington: ICS Publications, 1996), pp. 207–208.
18   Ibid., p. 194.

St. Thérèse, nicknamed "the little flower," continued to live her "Little Way" at Carmel. She lived it nobly and courageously, often in terrible pain and suffering, until her death. Trust and love are the key to the "Little Way," a gift that Thérèse has given to us all.

More than a half a century before Vatican II, Thérèse understood the primacy of the word of God and prepared the church for the teachings that the Scriptures should be open wide for all the faithful. In her own life, she acquired "the surpassing knowledge of Jesus Christ by frequent reading of the divine Scriptures."[19] Moreover, she united in her own heart a desire to love Jesus personally and a missionary desire to make him loved by others too. This harmony of prayerful listening to the word of God and the missionary impulse, practiced in every age of the church's renewal, prepared the way for the revival of lectio divina and for the New Evangelization in our day.

The Word of God in the New Evangelization

In this brief overview of the church in the first, sixth, thirteenth, sixteenth, and nineteenth centuries, we have seen that whenever the church goes through a period of renewal and evangelization, when the fire of the Spirit seems to be rekindled, it is associated with a renewed attention to sacred Scripture.

This pattern certainly holds for the church in our own day. The biblical renewal of the twentieth century that led to the Second Vatican Council unleashed a new awareness of the church's call to evangelize. Because the Council restored the word of God to its rightful place at the heart of the church's life, God's people throughout the world have recognized anew that the Christian vocation is both a call to the intimacy of discipleship with Jesus and to the apostolic impulse of mission. The renewed discovery of the ancient tradition of lectio divina in recent decades has formed a firm foundation for the New Evangelization.

Truly we are living in a new age of evangelizing renewal in the church, a period that began in the twentieth century and which will propel God's people through the coming decades of the twenty-first century. As more and more Catholics make reflective

_____

19   *Dei Verbum*, 25.

reading of Scripture a regular part of their lives as disciples of Jesus, we will see a new springtime in the church. Catholics will be more deeply evangelized so that we can become the evangelizers that Christ calls us to be.

For Reflection or Discussion

1. In what ways did Paul's years in Arabia after his conversion affect his evangelizing ministry?

2. How does the monastic life of St. Benedict inspire people today to listen and witness to the word of God?

3. What are some of the ways that St. Francis began a reform movement within the church of the Middle Ages?

4. How was the missionary fire in the heart of St. Dominic fueled by the Scriptures?

5. In what ways can the spirituality of St. Ignatius, expressed in *The Spiritual Exercises*, form evangelizing Catholics?

6. How is St. Thérèse an ideal model for the ways that meditation and contemplation of Scripture can transform the heart?

7. What are some key lessons we can learn from the saints as we seek to renew our lives as evangelizing Catholics today?

Chapter 3

Reading the Bible as Evangelizing Catholics

The longer we live and the wiser we become, the more we realize that so many things on which we try to build our lives are only temporary and fleeting. Those things in which we are tempted to put our hopes — like material possessions, physical pleasures, and worldly power — all prove ephemeral. They wither and fade. But, in contrast to this inevitable realization by every person at some point in life, God's word is enduring and eternal. As the prophet Isaiah proclaimed, "The grass withers, the flower fades, but the word of our God will stand forever" (Isa 40:8).

For Christian believers, what gives meaning to the world and purpose to life is the word of God. God has spoken his word in the history of salvation and revealed himself in deed and word to the people of Israel. This self-communication is expressed definitively in God's Son, in the life, death, and resurrection of Jesus Christ. In his first letter, Peter echoes and expands the words of Isaiah: "The word of the Lord endures forever. That word is the good news that was announced to you" (1 Pet 1:25).

Through the power and inspiration of the Holy Spirit, the word of God became flesh and the word of God became Scripture. This word of God has been entrusted to the church which then hands it on through the apostles and its apostolic tradition. The mission of the church is to proclaim the word of God to the world. Because Scripture is God's self-revelation and divinely inspired, we hear, read, experience, and share it with others as the word of God. And as the word of God, Scripture forms us into evangelizing disciples.

But how do we do this? How do we become biblical Catholics, evangelizing Catholics?

The more each of us engages in a prayerful and faith-filled reading of the Bible and thereby deepens our relationship with Jesus Christ, the more we are able to participate in the church's mission of evangelization — proclaiming the word of God to the world. We cannot keep to ourselves the word we have heard, the gospel we have received, the hope that is within us. Peter continues in his first letter, "Always be ready to make your defense to anyone who asks from you an account of the hope that is in you" (1 Pet 3:15).

For Christian believers, what gives meaning to the world and purpose to life is the word of God.

We are called to become evangelizing Catholics by first being evangelized ourselves by the word of God. Through prayerful, faith-filled, reflective reading of Scripture, we become people who communicate the gospel to others by the witness of our lives. By becoming biblical Catholics, we become ready to offer to others the reasons for the hope that lies within us, the gospel that animates our lives.

Peter's advice is often quoted by those who want Catholics to prove the church's teachings in opposition to all detractors. We must tell others about the hope that is in us, but sometimes we forget the rest of Peter's sentence: "yet do it with gentleness and reverence" (1 Pet 3:16). Our biblical understanding must never be used to pressure or overwhelm others. Our motivation for evangelization must always be love for others and a desire to help them remove whatever obstacles block the word of God from their lives.

Because Catholic evangelization must always be done with gentleness, respect, reverence, and love, we should follow the example of the saints throughout the centuries who modeled for us the way to hear the word of God in order to share the word of God. The best way to renew our faith, to be Catholic Christians in the twenty-first century, to be a part of the New Evangelization, is to learn how to read Scripture as the word of God. How do we read Scripture as the word of God so that we can become evangelizing

Christians? Here is what we have learned from the saints' lives and the church's rich tradition.

1) Listen for the Voice of God

God's self-revelation offered in Scripture is a personal reality. God gives us the inspired word in a revelatory way, in contrast to a merely informational way. The Scriptures are far more than an assembling of divine facts and truths. Because God is relational to the core, whatever is offered and received in Scripture, from beginning to end, is personal and relational. As stated in the Dogmatic Constitution on Divine Revelation, "In the sacred books the Father who is in heaven comes lovingly to meet his children, and talks with them."[20]

Because God's revelation is personal, we must be personally involved in God's self-communication. Every word we read, everything we see in our imagination as the narratives unfold, involves us relationally, pulls us into participation, and affects who we are and what we do. In the Bible we encounter God, and we are invited to ongoing conversion.

> **God gives us the inspired word in a revelatory way, in contrast to a merely informational way.**

Reading the Bible, then, in the tradition of the church and its saints, is a personal encounter with God. God speaks to his children, reveals his very self, and invites us to share in his divine life. Scripture is a privileged way in which we can come to know God more fully. God manifests himself to humanity through the long history of salvation which is expressed in the inspired Scriptures.

From beginning to end, from Genesis to Revelation, the Bible proclaims grace to the world, a grace beyond anything we could possibly hope or imagine. And the more we can open ourselves to God's life, the more we will be able to receive this divine gift. The traditional invitatory psalm of the church's Divine Office, Psalm 95, calls us to offer praise and thanksgiving to the Lord, and then

---

20   *Dei Verbum*, 21; CCC 104.

it invokes, "O that today you would listen to his voice!" (Ps 95:7). The work of today, indeed the work of our whole life, is to open our hearts anew to the living word of God.

Every time we open the Bible, our hearts should tremble a bit, wondering what we will hear as God speaks to us through the sacred text.

The saints of the church — Paul in the first century, Benedict in the sixth, Francis and Dominic in the thirteenth, Ignatius in the sixteenth, and Thérèse in the nineteenth — all discovered the Bible as a life-changing book because they heard there the voice of the Lord. I think of saints in our day as well: Dorothy Day, Pope John XXIII, Thomas Merton, Archbishop Romero, Pope John Paul II, Mother Teresa, and so many more. When they read the story of God in Scripture, they knew that it was this Lord, this invitation, this divine life that they desired with all their hearts.

Every time we open the Bible, our hearts should tremble a bit, wondering what we will hear as God speaks to us through the sacred text. We can prepare ourselves for each encounter by repeating the words of Samuel as we turn the pages: "Speak, LORD, for your servant is listening" (1 Sam 3:9–10). Some of the spiritual masters of old prayed and fasted before reading Scripture. Should we not at least invite God to open our ears and our hearts to truly listen to his word?

As the sacred book of the church, the Bible is a treasury of characters, stories, images, questions, prayers, and challenges. It preserves the hallowed memories of our Israelite and Christian ancestors. But Scripture is also a living word, a word filled with God's Spirit. And we believe that when we take this text in our hands, we encounter the word of God. We proclaim in liturgy, "The word of the Lord," "the gospel of the Lord." When we listen for the voice of the Lord, we can truly encounter God's word and respond in faith.

2) Trust in God's Inspiration

The early Christians understood that the sacred texts of Israel are "inspired." In the Greek text, the word is *theo-pneustos*, "God-breathed." Paul says, "All Scripture is inspired by God" (2 Tim 3:16). The teachings of the church expand this Pauline teaching to the complete Bible, expressing it this way: "The divinely revealed realities, which are contained and presented in the text of sacred Scripture, have been written down under the inspiration of the Holy Spirit."[21]

God's presence and life have somehow been breathed into sacred Scripture. God binds his own Spirit to these texts. The breath of divine life has been placed in these words. In these texts God is speaking, so much so that we can say that God is the truest author of Scripture.

Yet, at the same time, God chose certain human writers to inspire. Notice that Paul's word is *theo-pneustos*, "God-breathed," and not *theo-graptos*, "God-written." God did not write the words of the texts, nor did God dictate the words to human beings. Rather, as in the ancient prophets, "men and women moved by the Holy Spirit spoke from God" (2 Pet 1:21). As expressed by the Second Vatican Council, "God inspired the human authors of the sacred books.... God made full use of their own faculties and powers so that, though he acted in them and by them, it was as true authors that they consigned to writing whatever he wanted written, and no more."[22]

The Catholic tradition does not insist that every word of Scripture is historically, scientifically, and eternally exact.

Trusting in God's inspiration of Scripture means that we believe that the Bible is the word of God in human words. It means that we experience God's self-communication in a very human way, in a way we can understand. The Scriptures share in the incarnational reality of the Christian faith, in which the human and divine embrace. In the sacred texts, God reveals his own life and truth to humanity, but we experience it gradually through history, through human words and deeds, and through human authors and language. The Scriptures communicate God's life in a sacramental way, through the earthly material of humanity and of our world.

---

21   *Dei Verbum*, 11; CCC 105.
22   Ibid., 11; CCC 106.

So the language of the biblical texts is not capable of containing or fully capturing the fullness of God or of God's infinite truth. Yet, God does indeed communicate his word to us through the inspired Scriptures.

This understanding of the Bible's inspiration prevents the reader from falling into the distortions of fundamentalism. A tendency toward fundamentalism is a danger in every religion when interpreting its sacred texts. For Christians, a fundamentalist interpretation does not sufficiently take into account the incarnational reality of the Bible, the human authorship, and the historical origins and development of the Scriptures.

The Catholic tradition does not insist that every word of Scripture is historically, scientifically, and eternally exact. We must not hold these ancient texts to our contemporary definitions of accuracy. What God teaches in Scripture is truth — a reality that is far wider and deeper than our modern categories of fact and information. Here is Catholicism's current formulation of this teaching: "Since therefore all that the inspired authors affirm should be regarded as affirmed by the Holy Spirit, we must acknowledge that the books of Scripture firmly, faithfully, and without error teach that truth which God, for the sake of our salvation, wished to see confided to the Sacred Scriptures."[23] In other words, the truth that God desires to reveal through the inspired Scripture is "without error." The challenge, of course, for readers of the Bible and for the church is to discern what is the divine truth that God desires to reveal in a given passage of Scripture.

Catholic teaching stresses that texts must always be interpreted contextually — within their historical and cultural context, as well as within the context of the whole Bible and the church's ongoing tradition and teachings. A fundamentalist reading often lifts texts out of their context, placing undue stress on what they seem to say on the surface. So we can't just put the Bible into people's hands and say, "Read it." That's about as foolish as putting a set of car keys in a teenager's hands, pointing to a new car and saying, "Drive it." Reading the Bible can get us into trouble if we don't do it with guidance. Reading the Bible without a context

---

23   *Dei Verbum*, 11; CCC 107.

is typified by the fundamentalist bumper sticker: "God said it, I believe it, that settles it."

By understanding God's inspiration of Scripture, we can trust in the truth of biblical texts without trying to turn them into something they are not. Faithful study of the texts seeks to go beneath their surface to determine the essential and timeless points of the message. Because the Bible is inspired, it is trustworthy. It might not reveal the fullness of its truth automatically to every casual reader, but with time and in union with the church, we can trust the Bible to offer us the truth that God wants to reveal to us.

Through inspiration, Scripture is always youthful, offering us new insights, challenges, and truths.

Inspiration is not just what God did in the minds and hearts of the biblical writers thousands of years ago. God did indeed work within the human authors, but God continues to breathe within the inspired books. The sacred texts are always inspired; they are always filled with the Spirit of God. Because of the indwelling Spirit, the word is alive and charged with divine power to change and renew us. Because Scripture is inspired, the voice of God is heard, sounding through the biblical pages and into our hearts.

St. Jerome wrote that the Bible must be read and interpreted "in the light of the same Spirit by whom it was written."[24] A deep spiritual union is formed between the human author of the text, who was moved by the Spirit to write, and the prayerful reader of the inspired page, who is moved by that same Holy Spirit when reading it. The difference in time does not matter, because both are joined to the living word animated by the same Holy Spirit. Of course, the work of the human authors is finished, but because their words are penetrated by the life-giving Spirit, their writing is forever living.

Through inspiration, Scripture is always youthful, offering us new insights, challenges, and truths. The Holy Spirit continues to breathe life and power into the sacred texts, so that on every

---

24   Jerome, *Commentaries on the Letter to the Galatians* 5, 19–21: *Patrologia Latina* 26, 417a.

page we can truly encounter the living word of God. God meets us on the holy ground of these pages. In every line, the voice of God whispers: Look, I am here. I am breathing in these sacred texts, and I am breathing within you.

3) Understand the One Story of Salvation

Although the Bible consists of a variety of books and types of literature, it offers us one unfolding drama. It is essentially the narrative of God's redemption of the world, set against the backdrop of God's design for creation and of human rebellion. Prophets, judges, kings, priests, apostles, and evangelists belong to the one story of salvation.

This biblical account of the world's redemption encompasses the whole world and offers us God's intentions and desires that give meaning and purpose to human life. The one story of salvation invites us into a grand narrative, explaining for us the way things are, how they have come to be so, and what they will ultimately be. It begins with creation and ends with the renewal of all things in the new creation for which we are destined. And in between, it offers us an interpretation of the whole of human history. Learning to take a panoramic view of the Bible enables us to live in the narrative and discover the real story of which each of our lives are a part.

At God's invitation and command, we participate in God's own mission to redeem all creation and to restore the world to God's gracious rule.

In the Old Testament, God gathers Israel into his divine purpose for the world and chooses this people to reveal God to the other nations. God commissioned Israel to demonstrate to the other nations what it meant to be in covenant with God and to live under God's gracious rule. As a light to the nations, Israel would bring God's redemptive blessings to the world. Yet, Israel's continual infidelity to this call and covenant led to God's offer of a new covenant mediated by Jesus the Messiah. Through his apostles, Jesus gathers and restores Israel to their calling in the world. This nucleus of renewed Israel is commissioned to continue the mission of Jesus to the ends of the earth, gathering all nations into God's covenant to live under God's rule and blessings.

The time between the coming of Christ and his coming again to restore all things is characterized by the evangelizing mission of the apostolic church. It is the appointed time for the church's witness to the ends of the earth. Our identity as God's people is rooted in that biblical task of extending the offer of God's salvation to all. At God's invitation and command, we participate in God's own mission to redeem all creation and to restore the world to God's gracious rule. We are sent with the good news to announce with our words, demonstrate with our deeds, and embody in our lives God's new creation and end-time salvation.

N. T. Wright describes the Bible and our role within it with an analogy. He imagines that the script of a lost Shakespearean play is somehow discovered. Although the play originally had five acts, only a little more than four have been found — the first four acts and the first scene of act five. The rest is missing. The play is given to Shakespearian actors who are asked to work out the rest of act five for themselves. Immersing themselves in Shakespearean language and in the narrative of the partial script that has been recovered, they improvise the missing part of the fifth act, allowing their performance to be shaped by the trajectory of the story as they have come to understand it. In this way they bring the play toward the conclusion that its author had indicated previously in the play.

Wright says that this analogy may help us to understand how the Bible can shape our own lives now. The biblical drama of redemption unfolds in five acts: 1) creation, 2) the fall into sin, 3) Israel's story, 4) the story of Jesus Christ, and 5) the story of the church, leading to the consummation of God's plan of redemption. We know that the Author of the drama, the Divine "Playwright," has given the gift of his own Spirit to the "actors." So, we must live our lives within the trajectory of the story as it has been told up to the first part of the final act. We have been entrusted to perform the continuation of the biblical drama within the mission

of Jesus and his church, moving the story forward to the conclusion that God has already imagined.[25]

**We have shattered the Bible into fragments: moral pieces,
doctrinal pieces, lectionary pieces, and devotional pieces.**

This unfinished drama of salvation, containing its own plot,
impetus, and motion, demands that those who enter it bring it to
a satisfactory conclusion. We are invited to freely and responsibly
enter into the plot as it stands, continually poring over and immersing ourselves in the earlier acts, and learning to understand
how the threads could be drawn together. We then improvise,
speaking and acting creatively, yet in a way consistent with the
story of Israel, Jesus, and the early church. We each imaginatively
yet faithfully live out the narrative impetus given in Scripture in
the new historical and cultural situations in which our lives are
placed by God.

This analogy does not mean that the Bible is a tightly woven
narrative with a single story line, as we might expect with a modern biography or a conventional novel. It is a mixture of lots of
narratives as well as many other types of literature. In the Bible we
find history, poetry, parables, proverbs, prayers, songs, legal codes,
genealogies, apocalypses, and many other literary forms. Each type
of literature must be interpreted in a way that is appropriate to its
genre, but every part finds its full meaning only in the context of
the whole Bible. And when we look at the Bible as one overarching and all-encompassing story of salvation, we can see its overall
direction and understand the place of its many parts.

We have shattered the Bible into fragments: moral pieces,
doctrinal pieces, lectionary pieces, and devotional pieces. When
we break up the Bible in this way, it loses its power to form culture and to mold our lives in a comprehensive way. It becomes
a series of teaching stories, proof texts, homiletic material, and
prayer bits. Of course, there is nothing wrong with using the Bi-

---

25   N. T. Wright, *The New Testament and the People of God*
(Minneapolis: Fortress Press, 1992), p. 143.

ble in any of these ways, but we must always keep in mind the full context of these biblical fragments. They are parts of a larger whole, God's revelation of his intentions for humanity. When we lose sight of the story of Israel, Jesus, and the church, we have lost the plot.

The Bible is indeed a wonderful library of seventy-three books. But all of this wonderful variety of books forms one tradition and is encompassed in one Bible. This essential library of the descendants of Abraham is the book of the church. When we understand that the Bible is our literature, we enter into the story ourselves and we view our lives as participants in the grand narrative of salvation. The more that we can understand the whole Bible as the one great drama of salvation, from creation to new creation, and then find ourselves within that great story, the better we will embody Scripture and become participants in the mission of God.

4) Discover the Book of Christ

The mystery of Jesus Christ is the center and focus of the whole Christian Bible. He is the key that opens up the full meaning of all parts of Scripture. The Bible is, above all else, the book of Christ. This is the way most Christians have read the Bible over the past two thousand years.

Jesus himself taught his disciples to see the rich continuity of God's plan of salvation and to appreciate how all of Israel's history pointed to his coming. These teachings came to a climactic moment when the risen Lord appeared to his disciples on the road to Emmaus. Luke tells us, "Then beginning with Moses and all the prophets, he interpreted to them the things about himself in all the scriptures" (Lk 24:27).

The death and resurrection of the Lord sheds new light on the Old Testament texts and enriches them with new meaning. This is why Paul of Tarsus, after encountering the risen Lord, had to go east to Arabia in order to read the ancient texts again in the new light of Christ. Only together do the Old and New Testaments express God's full revelation. As St. Augustine said, "The New Testament lies hidden in the Old, and the Old Testament is unveiled in the New."[26] We can come to understand the Old Testament fully only when we see it as a mother who bears the New Testament in her womb and gives birth to it.

Because we are believers and because the Holy Spirit works within us, we can see Christ whenever we read a page of sacred Scripture.

Of course we can read and interpret the texts of the Old Testament as the literature of Israel and appreciate their value in and of themselves. We can be grateful for these books in their Jewish context and learn from them. Likewise we can read the New Testament alone, and understand it as the story of Jesus and the early church. But for the Christian believer, the two testaments must be read in light of one another because they form one book in which the mystery of Christ is the focal center.

In the Acts of the Apostles, Philip encounters the Ethiopian in his chariot reading from the prophet Isaiah. Philip asks the man if he understands what he is reading, and the Ethiopian admits that he needs some help. He invites Philip into his chariot and asks him about whom the prophet was speaking. The text then says: "Then Philip began to speak, and starting with this Scripture, he proclaimed to him the good news about Jesus" (Acts 8:35). The meaning of Scripture is richer and fuller than could have been understood by the original human writers. Although Isaiah's words may have made sense to his Israelite hearers in their historical context, their meaning is most complete in the light of Christ. We see this same pattern throughout Acts, especially in the speeches of Peter and Paul. They quote continually from the Old Testament to proclaim how Jesus is the climax of God's saving plan for the world.

To those who refused to accept him, Jesus said, "If you believed Moses, you would believe me, for he wrote about me" (Jn 5:46). With these words, Jesus proclaimed that the whole Torah is ultimately about himself. Eventually, those who came to believe in him would recognize his presence throughout the Scriptures.

---

26 Augustine, *Quaestiones in heptateuchum* 2, 73: *Patrologia Latina* 34, 623.

Because we are believers and because the Holy Spirit works within us, we can see Christ whenever we read a page of sacred Scripture. As Hugh of St. Victor from the twelfth century says so beautifully,

> All sacred Scripture is but one book, and this one book is Christ; because all sacred Scripture speaks of Christ, and all sacred Scripture is fulfilled in Christ.[27]

In the whole Bible, in all of its parts, we can experience an encounter with God in Christ. Colossians says, "[Christ] is the image of the invisible God, the firstborn of all creation.... All things were created through him and for him" (Col 1:15–16). He is the reason for all reality and the destination of history, the Alpha and Omega. In his divine eternity, God spoke only one Word: "In the beginning was the Word, and the Word was with God, and the Word was God" (Jn 1:1).

Before Christ came into the world, however, that word expressed itself in many different ways, multiplied throughout the Scriptures of Israel. God communicated his message of salvation in various and partial ways through the voices of many inspired writers. But when the fullness of time came, the Word returned to its original unity: "The Word became flesh and lived among us" (Jn 1:14). Now God speaks to us through Christ:

> Long ago God spoke to our ancestors in many and various ways by the prophets, but in these last days he has spoken to us by a Son, whom he appointed heir of all things. (Heb 1:1–2)

The many words became the one Word, the living Word to which every other word bears witness. God's Word is now not only audible but visible and tangible, now not only spoken but incarnate and living. Christ, the Word made flesh, has traditionally been called the *Verbum abbreviatum*, the "abbreviated Word." In Christ, the many parts of the Bible are harmonized and unified. John of the Cross put it succinctly in *The Ascent of Mount Carmel*: "In giving us his Son, Who is his only Word, God has said everything to

---

27   Hugh of St. Victor, *The Ark of Noah*, 2, 8: *Patrologia Latina* 176, 642c.

us at once, in one simple stroke, in this single word — and he has nothing more to say."[28]

Meditating on Scripture, then, is not so much a matter of interpreting a book as of seeking Someone. The meaning we find in Scripture is not impersonal truth but ultimately the person of Christ. For this reason, lectio divina is not primarily an intellectual exercise but a devoted and passionate search, an enthusiastic and joyful discovery.

5) Search for Beauty

For the masses of Christians through the ages, most of whom have been illiterate and unable to read the biblical texts, church art and architecture have displayed the biblical story of salvation. Byzantine mosaics display the scenes of Scripture in a wondrous way, and Gothic cathedrals present the Bible in stone and glass.

But the Bible itself is also beautiful. Its literature is far more captivating than an ancient basilica. When we search for the beauty in the sacred pages, we can experience the splendor of the word of God.

By emphasizing truth and goodness in the Bible, we try to make Christianity persuasive, as we should. But we also need a corresponding emphasis on beauty to make Christianity attractive.

The Greek philosophers and the church fathers spoke of three prime virtues: truth, goodness, and beauty. As prime virtues, they need no further justification — they are their own justification, which is a way of saying that truth, goodness, and beauty don't need to be made practical — they don't have to do anything to be of value. Their value is inherent; we simply choose them because they are true, good, and beautiful.

The early theologians located the source of these prime virtues as proceeding from God himself because God is true, good,

---

28   Adapted from *The Ascent of Mt. Carmel*, 22, 3, in *The Works of St. John of the Cross* (London: Hasell, Watson & Viney, Ltd., 1922).

and beautiful. So these virtues become a guide to Christian living as we seek to believe what is true, become what is good, and behold what is beautiful.

We are used to seeking truth in Scripture, and we often interpret the Bible as a guide to goodness. But it is the third virtue, the virtue of beauty, which has been most deemphasized in the way we understand the faith. As a result, Christianity has suffered a loss of beauty — a loss that needs to be recovered.

By emphasizing truth and goodness in the Bible, we try to make Christianity persuasive, as we should. But we also need a corresponding emphasis on beauty to make Christianity attractive. Evangelization should not only seek to persuade with truth and goodness, but it should also attract with beauty. We need to present the faith as something beautiful. Sometimes where truth and goodness cannot convince, beauty can entice.

We must learn to come to the Bible like an Orthodox worshipper approaches an icon. The believer looks at the icon from the outside and is drawn into it. The face, gestures, movement, and colors invite the believer to step into a fuller reality than our material world. Contemplating with an icon is an experience of being drawn into the kingdom of heaven where Christ and the saints dwell, where the saving deeds of Christ are received by the Father, and where the saving mysteries of the faith are eternal.

Meditating on Scripture is a very similar experience. The inspired text draws us in. The characters and the scenes capture our imaginations and invite us into their world. Through the Holy Spirit alive in the text and within us, the Scriptures breathe God's truth, goodness, and beauty. As God's living word, they captivate us and move us toward God's grace, to share in the divine life. The Bible is not just a collection of sentimental sayings, as it is sometimes presented in the West. Rather, like genuine beauty, it is mysterious, dangerous, fascinating, and awesome. As beauty awakens our spirit and opens us to transcendence, the Bible can bring us into the presence of God.

In creating biblical art, the artist interprets the text in such a way as to produce a beautiful work. It is the artist's spiritual vision and profound meditation on the word of God that produces great art. But all believers can meditate on the text, ponder its meaning, and produce a beautiful life. As art grows within the imagination of the Christian artist in response to Scripture, so saints grow within the womb of the church through their response to God's word. And just as a beautiful work of art can evangelize, our lives can announce the good news by the ways we respond to the beauty we discover in the word of God. As Christian art can be a visual gospel, we too can be God's work of art by reflecting and witnessing to God's saving love.

We've got to learn how to see the beauty in the word of God, no matter the media.

But we have to develop our Christian sense of beauty, because the standards of the world are not the Christian standards for beauty. Genuine beauty appeals to the soul. For example, the crucifix, in the eyes of the world, is ugly and scandalous. But for the Christian, the crucifix is beautiful to behold. The tortured body of Jesus, his arms outstretched in loving embrace of the world, expresses the beauty that saves the world. The crucifix hanging in churches across the world is a biblical commentary, announcing that if Christ can transform the Roman instrument of physical torture and psychological terror into a thing of beauty, then there is hope that in Christ all things can be made beautiful. The beauty of our crucified Lord expresses the wondrous reality that God has entered into the deepest pains of our world and proclaimed resurrection, inviting us to enter deeply into our brutal world with hope and confidence in God's eternal love.

The monks throughout the Christian centuries created illuminated pages of Scripture to express the beauty of God's word. In the scriptoriums of their monasteries, they meticulously copied the pages of the sacred text onto fine parchment, and they illuminated the pages with gold leaf, brilliant colors, and exquisite miniature art. These illuminated pages are a wonderful expression of the beauty of Scripture, and when we see them in museums today, we are stirred by the devotion of the ancients.

Although we have paperback Bibles and Bible apps today, the same words, the same text, the same inspired Scripture is contained in these modern media as in the ancient manuscripts. We've got to learn how to see the beauty in the word of God, no matter the media. Through paper and ink or digital texts, the word of God can captivate us and entice us. The images, metaphors, stories, adventures, symbols, poetry, songs, and prayers of Scripture are beautiful because they express Christ, who is Divine Beauty Incarnate, and draw us into the kingdom of God.

6) Experience Scripture with Your Whole Self

The human person is an embodied spirit. We respond to God's revelation with our intellect, memory, will, emotions, senses, imagination, drives, and desires. Reading Scripture as the word of God requires that we bring the entirety of our being to the practice. Conversion and growth in discipleship is a lifelong process that engages the whole human person.

In the ancient world, the reading of Scripture was always done aloud. Even when the reading was in private, the readers would always move their lips and vocalize the text. In this way, they saw the text with their eyes, pronounced the text with their lips, and heard the text with their ears. In this way, a range of senses is employed in reading Scripture. The spiritual masters always taught that the more senses we can involve in our spiritual practices, the more effectively we will experience the divine. For this reason, the use of candles, incense, and other sensual stimuli can enhance our experience of the sacred text as the word of God.

> Scripture nourishes our embodied spirits as food nourishes our physical bodies. For this reason, we don't just study Scripture; we assimilate it.

But more than involving our senses, we should strive to read Scripture as insiders, as participants in the world of the Bible, and not simply as outsiders, looking in from a distance. This means allowing the scenes to become real in our imagination. It means allowing the feelings and emotions expressed in the text to interact with our own. It means acquiring an experiential knowledge of the text, rather than simply an intellectual understanding.

This kind of inside reading leads us to respond from within the world of the text. As a participant in the biblical world, we bring our whole self to the reading, with both our minds and our hearts engaged. The goal of this holistic reading of Scripture is an encounter with God. The experience of reading Scripture as the word of God leads us to a dialogue with God: first we listen to God speak through his word, and then we respond to God as a reply to this encounter.

For example, when we read Scripture, we can come to an intellectual knowledge that God loves us, based on the abstract truths that we discover in the text. Yet, although we know with our head that God loves us, sometimes our heart tells us that God just, well, tolerates us. But then we begin to read the biblical narratives from the inside, especially scenes in which Jesus encounters suffering, sinful, struggling people; we allow the truth of God's love to be experienced in our heart. When Jesus looks up at Zacchaeus peering at him from the tree limb and says, "I must stay at your house today," the heart of Jesus is longing to encounter Zacchaeus in a way that will transform his life. And indeed, Zacchaeus's life was turned inside out by that encounter because he discovered that his corruption and many failures were no barrier to the love of God that he had experienced in Jesus. In actions more than words, Jesus told Zacchaeus that God yearns for him and longs to be with him. Right now, despite his sins, God is drawing near to him with love. When we soak in narratives like this with our whole self, we can know with our mind and our heart, feel with our emotions and our desires, and truly experience God changing our lives.

Scripture nourishes our embodied spirits as food nourishes our physical bodies. For this reason, we don't just study Scripture; we assimilate it. We take it in, eat it, chew it, digest it, and we get those words flowing through our bloodstream. The prophet Ezekiel tells about his vision of God in which the divine being handed him a scroll written on both sides and tells him to eat the scroll.

> He said to me, O mortal, eat what is offered to you; eat this scroll, and go, speak to the house of Israel. So I opened my mouth, and he gave me the scroll to eat. He said to me, Mortal, eat this scroll that I give you and fill your stomach with

it. Then I ate it; and in my mouth it was as sweet as honey. He said to me: Mortal, go to the house of Israel and speak my very words to them. (Ezek 3:1–4)

God placed his own word into his prophet so that it could become enfleshed in him. God wanted Ezekiel to experience his word with his whole self so that he could genuinely proclaim that word to others. Likewise, God wants us to experience Scripture deeply so that his word may be digested and nourish our lives. We assimilate Scripture so that it becomes metabolized in works of healing, service, justice, and forgiveness. The sacred text is then transformed through us with God's grace into witness and evangelization.

7) Develop a Biblical Imagination

Encouraging his listeners to live the Christian life, Paul urges, "Let the same mind be in you that was in Christ Jesus" (Phil 2:5). He wants them to be formed in such a way that they can truly say, "We have the mind of Christ" (1 Cor 2:16). Putting on the mind of Christ means taking on his way of thinking, his attitude, and his understanding of life. We could say that putting on the mind of Christ is the way to live the Christian life.

God speaks to us in our imaginations, and through our imaginations we open ourselves more fully to the spiritual reality of God's life and promises.

Our Catholic tradition teaches us that the best way to take on Christ's way of thinking about life is to reflectively read the Scriptures. When we read the narratives of the Hebrew Scriptures, for example, we listen to the stories of Israel's ancestors that formed the mind-set of Jesus. When we read the psalms, we are hearing the prayers that formed the heart of Jesus, the chants of the temple and synagogue that formed Jesus' prayers to the Father. When we read the prophets, we hear the words that molded Jesus' understanding of his own mission to God's people. Thus, absorbing our minds in the Old Testament shapes our attitudes and understandings to be like that of Christ.

Likewise, meditating on the four gospels, the Acts of the Apostles, and the letters of the New Testament forms our minds to be like that of Christ. When we read the life of Jesus, imagine his saving deeds, listen to his teachings, and hear about the work of his Holy Spirit in the lives of his followers, we fill our own imaginations with the words, images, and vision of life that filled the mind of Jesus Christ.

Putting on the mind of Christ and living in him means developing a biblical imagination. When we exercise our imagination, our minds and our hearts work together to create images. The life of faith requires using our imagination to create images and concepts that we can't tangibly experience with our five senses. Actually what the five senses are to our physical bodies, the imagination is to our embodied spirit. The imagination is the gateway to spiritual experiences that are more real than what we can experience only in the material world.

There has been an unfortunate de-emphasis on the important role of the imagination in the past couple of centuries. Our rationalistic modern world has convinced us that anything we might experience in our imagination is just fanciful and unreal. Yet, God speaks to us in our imaginations, and through our imaginations we open ourselves more fully to the spiritual reality of God's life and promises. We experience Scripture with our whole self when we engage our imagination, the senses of the soul.

Our Christian imagination is enriched when we spend time dwelling in the Scriptures. When we engage both our minds and our hearts in regular, reflective reading of the Bible, we submit our imagination to the work of God's Spirit and we gradually become filled with the images of divine life and we develop a biblical imagination.

When we read Isaiah, for instance, we imagine Isaiah's vision in the temple, and hear the seraphim calling out: "Holy, holy, holy is the LORD of hosts; the whole earth is full of his glory" (Isa 6:3). And when these images present themselves to our soul, we begin to catch more glimpses of God's glory reflected in the tangible experiences of the sunrise, the waterfall, and the eagle's flight. We realize that the whole earth is charged with God's grandeur. Then we continue reading and find an extraordinary vision of a world healed by God's love, a world in which the wolf and the lamb lie together in peace, a world of reconciliation and harmony, where the swords for making war are transformed to plowshares for making peace. So with a soul filled with hope, we know that we must live between this world, filled with reflections of God's glory, and a future in which all that disfigures God's design is done away with and the glorious presence of God renews the whole creation.

When the biblical prophets looked around them, they saw only idolatry and injustice. Yet they did not despair but called people to hope. Their continual refrain was "The day is coming," a day when God will rule, injustice will cease, evil will be made right, and God's people will experience the deliverance for which they have hoped. Their message required that their hearers in Israel form images and concepts in their imaginations contrary to what they experienced with their senses. The prophets shaped the imaginations of God's people with the truths and promises that God revealed.

A biblical imagination, filled with supernatural imagery and inspired revelation, is part of God's gift for our redeemed humanity.

Jesus calls his followers to an even greater act of imagination. While the prophets promised, "The day is coming," Jesus proclaims, "The day has come." The day the prophets envisioned has come upon us. Jesus taught that the kingdom of God is at hand, and he told parables to express what the kingdom is like. He filled the imaginations of his disciples, enabling them to see the reality of God's reign in the world beneath the appearances of human experience.

When the scribe asked Jesus what he must do to receive eternal life, Jesus asked him about the commandments of the law. The scribe answered correctly when he repeated the two great commands to love God and neighbor. Although he tried to trap Jesus with a technical question, "Who is my neighbor?" Jesus replied with a story in order to drive the question beyond the intellectual realm and into the heart. With the unforgettable parable of the Good Samaritan, Jesus enriched the scribe's imagination and that of his whole church. Jesus was not just concerned that his followers know his teachings, but that they actually follow in his way. His final words were, "Go and do likewise" (Lk 10:37).

A biblical imagination, filled with supernatural imagery and inspired revelation, is part of God's gift for our redeemed humanity. Such an imagination refuses to limit truth to what can be perceived with the senses, but understands divine truth, which enlarges our horizons and broadens our perspectives. An imagination nourished with Scripture knows that Incarnation and Resurrection are real and that divine life is our destiny. It enables us to live within the great story of salvation, a grand vision of reality, from creation to the new creation when God will bring earth and heaven together finally and forever. In this world today, with all its present ugliness and pain, we are called to put on the mind of Christ, to embody his gospel, and to be agents of the new creation. We can live as his disciples because we know that the kingdom of God is upon us and the new creation has broken into our world with healing and redemption. It enables us to inhabit a world where God reigns, where evil has been conquered, where sinners have been redeemed, and where Christ is seated at God's right hand in glory.

Disciples who have put on the mind of Christ evangelize naturally. Because they have developed a biblical imagination, they witness God's reign to those around them. These evangelizing disciples experience glimpses of God's glory, act with justice even when it does them no earthly good, and bear witness to the gospel in word and deed.

8) Read with Expectation

Because the inspired Scriptures express God's living word, we know that they contain a powerful inner dynamic. The word of God is potent because it communicates God's healing strength and his saving authority. The divine word creates change within those who read it with this expectation. Jeremiah declared that God's word is like fire and like a hammer that breaks a rock in pieces (Jer 23:29). The psalmist says that God's word is "a lamp to my feet and a light to my path," a luminous beacon guiding our way through life's darkness (Ps 119:105). Jesus said that God's word is like seed planted in soil, and when the rocks and thorns are removed, it yields an abundant harvest (Mk 4:14). The writer of Hebrews proclaims, "The word of God is living and active, sharper than any two-edged sword," penetrating into the deepest parts of our being (Heb 4:12).

The Bible presents us with a vast, intricate, magnificent spiritual place, filled with stories, ideas, songs, poetry, prophecy, and more, within which we can walk and dwell with God.

When Moses saw the burning bush, God said to him, "Take off your shoes, for this is holy ground." God wanted Moses to prepare himself and to be ready for this divine encounter. When we read the Bible, we are like Moses before the burning bush. The word of God is fiery but never consumed, effective and never depleted. God wanted Moses to take off his sandals, to plant his feet firmly in the earth, and prepare himself for the experience he was about to undergo. When we read the Bible with this kind of expectation, we will experience a true encounter with God. And when we truly believe that we encounter God as we read and meditate on the sacred page, then we can expect to be changed in some way by that encounter.

Reading the Bible with expectation leads us to experience what is called in Celtic spirituality "a thin place." A thin place is a situation in which the boundary between heaven and earth is especially thin, a place where we can sense the divine more readily. And thin places are generally beautiful places. The Bible speaks about a lot of thin places. Certainly Moses' encounter with God at the burning bush was a thin place. Mountains in the Bible are thin places. The meeting tent in the desert and the temple in Jerusalem are thin places. For Catholics, the sacraments, especially Eucharist, are thin places. And we can learn to experience the Bible as a thin place, a place where we can experience God more readily, a place where heaven and earth come close together.

The Bible presents us with a vast, intricate, magnificent spiritual place, filled with stories, ideas, songs, poetry, prophecy, and more, within which we can walk and dwell with God. This holy ground is not a place where we can occasionally visit or peer in from afar. The world of Scripture is our sacred place, the book of God's people, the story of salvation which God is continually shaping. We must bring ourselves into the text, to be participants within this sacred space, to continually encounter our God in this thin place.

The whole Bible, from beginning to end, proclaims God's grace to the world.

Reading with expectation means that we fully expect to encounter God in his inspired word, that we expect God to reveal his presence, his wisdom, his way as we read. It means that we read the Bible with empty hands, placing the control in God's hands rather than our own. Reading with expectation means truly listening, knowing that God's agenda may be different from our own. It means learning how to read the Bible in a way that doesn't require that we have all the answers, but that requires us to stay present to the text as it makes us present to the great mystery of God.

In order to read the Bible with expectation, we must have a deep desire for God. Yet, at the same time, we realize that our longing for God is a result of God's deep desire for us. God's grace creates this longing within us. It is this desire for God that creates the listening ear, the open hands, and the receptive heart that are so necessary to hear God's word in Scripture. When we desire God and are ready for his presence, we will read Scripture with expectation, and God's word will invite us into a deeper relationship with him.

The whole Bible, from beginning to end, proclaims God's grace to the world. God draws near to his people while we are still sinners and delights in us. Genesis to Revelation speaks of God's great yearning for us, and it inspires within us a yearning to be in his presence. The Bible opens us to the healing and transforming power of God's grace. God doesn't just throw us back on our own meager resources to change ourselves so that he can then love us. God has a passionate desire for us. And knowing God's desire for us makes us expectant, wanting to know his will for us, trusting that he will change us, open to whatever he wants of us.

9) Celebrate the Word in Union with the Sacraments

Biblical mosaics, paintings, and stained glass can certainly be appreciated on the wall of museums, but when they are incorporated into the churches for which they were created, they express their original purposefulness. Likewise, when sacred music is performed in a concert hall, it can certainly be beautiful and uplifting, but when it is integrated into the church's liturgy, it becomes part of the worship of God's people for which it was composed. The same is true with the Bible. We can read Scripture with genuine appreciation as great literature. We can read it also in prayerful and reflective study, and experience it as God's word. But when the Scriptures are read or chanted in the liturgy of the church, the word of the Lord attains its fullest realization.

The tradition of Israel and the church demonstrates the unity of Scripture and liturgy. The gathered community of God's people is the most natural setting for sacred Scripture because, by and large, the texts were written for communal worship. In the liturgy, the sacred texts are proclaimed and "actualized." The Scriptures usher the worshippers into the liturgical action, and the word of God is made alive and effective for the worshippers.[29]

The Mass and all the sacraments of the church are formed from the Scriptures and by the Scriptures.

The proclamation of God's word within the assembly has always been a necessary part of the praise, thanksgiving, and sacrificial worship of God's people. In the celebration of Israel's Sabbaths and feasts, the Scriptures were proclaimed and chanted in the temple, synagogues, and homes. The covenant with God was periodically renewed by gathering the people, reading from the scrolls of God's revelation preserved in the sanctuary, and offering sacrifice.

Likewise, for the early Christians, the assembly gathered for instruction and worship was the primary place in which God's people heard the Scriptures. In word and sacrament, believers were

---

29   See Scott Hahn, *Letter and Spirit: From Written Text to Living Word in the Liturgy* (New York: Doubleday, 2005).

baptized into Christ and experienced his risen life in Eucharist. And the texts of the New Testament were created, proclaimed, and canonized within the context of the church's liturgy. The apostles wrote letters to be read in the church when the believers gathered on the Lord's Day. Soon after being written, the four gospels were proclaimed in the Eucharistic liturgy of the church. Both the books of the Old and New Testaments were selected and canonized not so much for private study as for liturgical reading. The list of books that eventually formed the complete Bible were those most fit for use in the church's public worship. The councils of the church essentially ratified the canon of Scripture that was being read in the worship and sacramental life of the church.

The Mass and all the sacraments of the church are formed from the Scriptures and by the Scriptures. All the parts of the liturgy, the ritual words and the ritual actions, find their origin in the Scriptures of Israel and the apostolic Scriptures of the church. When we consider the form and vocabulary of the introductory rites, the Liturgy of the Word and Eucharist, and the closing rites and blessings, as well as the rituals of the seven sacraments, we see that they are all drawn from the Bible.[30]

This unity of Scripture and Eucharistic worship is demonstrated in Luke's Emmaus account. We first see that along the journey to Emmaus, the risen Jesus is present with his disciples, opening the Scriptures to them: "Then beginning with Moses and all the prophets, he interpreted to them the things about himself in all the Scriptures" (Lk 24:27). He shows how all the ancient texts come to their completion in him, joining Israel's covenant with his climactic death and resurrection. Then, at table, Jesus becomes known to the disciples in the breaking of the bread. The interrelationship between opening the Scriptures and the breaking of the bread, the liturgy of the word flowing into the liturgy of the Eucharist, forms the structure of the church's Eucharistic liturgy through the ages.

---

30   See Stephen J. Binz, *The Mass in Scripture* (Huntington, IN: Our Sunday Visitor, 2011), *The Sacraments in Scripture* (Huntington, IN: Our Sunday Visitor, 2011), and *The Creed in Scripture* (Huntington, IN: Our Sunday Visitor, 2012).

From the Reformation in the sixteenth century until recent decades, Catholic practice has focused on the real presence of Christ's body and blood in the Eucharistic elements, because of challenges to the church's sacramental teachings. But in the earlier liturgy of the church, the transforming power of Scripture and its authority as God's word received as much emphasis as Christ's sacramental presence. As bread and wine are transformed into Christ's body and blood, Scripture is transformed into the living word. Both word and sacrament make Christ present to us; both give spiritual nourishment to God's people.

Origen, writing in the third century, indicates the belief of the early church in both the real presence of Christ in the Eucharist and the transforming power of the inspired Scriptures:

> You are accustomed to take part in the divine mysteries, so you know how, when you have received the body of the Lord, you reverently exercise every care lest a particle of it fall and lest anything of the consecrated gift perish. You account yourselves guilty, and rightly do you so believe, if any of it be lost through negligence. But if you are so careful to preserve his body, and rightly so, why do you think that there is less guilt to have neglected God's word than to have neglected his body.[31]

The implementation of the documents of the Second Vatican Council has restored this ancient parallelism between the Scriptures and the Eucharist. In many churches of our day, the Scriptures are enthroned for veneration in a similar way as the sacrament is reserved in the tabernacle. In today's liturgy, we often bring candles and incense to the ambo where the Scriptures are proclaimed, as well as to the altar. The ordained minister bows, crosses himself, and kisses the book — gestures of reverence signifying that Christ is present in the gospels as well as at the sacrament of the altar. When the gospels are proclaimed, worshippers greet the presence of the Lord with the words, "Glory to you, O Lord."

St. Jerome, in the fourth century, reminds us that Scripture is a real encounter with Christ. He exhorts his listeners to satisfy

---

31   Origen, *On Exodus*, 13.3.

their hungers and quench their thirsts through Eucharistic communion and through the reading of Scripture:

> Since the Lord's flesh is real food and his blood real drink ... our only good in the present age is to eat his flesh and drink his blood, not only in the Eucharistic mystery but also in the reading of Scripture.[32]

The Mass, we might say, is the Bible in action, the saving truths and events of Scripture made present and real before us in the Eucharistic liturgy.

This unity of the word of God and the Eucharistic presence of Christ is expressed by the dual emphasis of the *Dogmatic Constitution on Divine Revelation*. Both are to be venerated by the faithful, since they each nourish God's people as the bread of life:

> The church has always venerated the divine Scriptures just as she venerated the Body of the Lord, in so far as she never ceases, particularly in the sacred liturgy, to partake of the bread of life and to offer it to the faithful from the one table of the word of God and the Body of Christ.[33]

Both word and sacrament are necessary for the full expression of Christ's presence with his church. The Mass, we might say, is the Bible in action, the saving truths and events of Scripture made present and real before us in the Eucharistic liturgy. A sacrament, as Augustine said, is a *visibile verbum*,[34] "a visible word." The sacramental rite enacts within the believing assembly the deepest sense of the proclaimed word.

What the individual experiences in lectio divina, the worshipping assembly experiences in the Mass. The individual receives God's word, meditating on it and assimilating it, then the believer responds to God's word in prayer, contemplation, and witness.

---

32   Jerome, *Commentary on Ecclesiastes*, 3: *Patrologia Latina* 23, 1039a.

33   *Dei Verbum*, 21; CCC 103.

34   Augustine, *Tractatus in evangelium Iohannis*, 80, 3.

Likewise, in the Eucharistic ritual, Christ speaks to his church and we respond in worship and in action on behalf of the world. In this way, lectio divina leads to and flows from the liturgy of the church.

The church's Eucharistic liturgy won't let us read our Bible individualistically. We can't just join with our Bible study friends each week and let it go at that. The liturgy brings us into a confrontation with God's word in the company of the people of God throughout time and space — joining us with the angels and saints, and with brothers and sisters throughout the world — listening and responding to God's living word.

Then, after joining us together, the liturgy sends us out, to proclaim with our lives the reality we have experienced. "Go and announce the gospel of the Lord" and "Go in peace, glorifying the Lord by your life" — these are two of the closing acclamations by which we are sent out from the Mass and into the world. After celebrating the Lord's presence in word and sacrament, we are commissioned to go forth and evangelize.

10) Expect to Become an Evangelizer

The church's liturgy has two primary movements. First, it brings people from the world into the sanctuary for communal worship, gathering them to listen, believe, and receive. Then, it moves people out of the sanctuary and back into the world. Having encountered Christ in word and sacrament, we travel back to the places where we spend our lives to witness and to serve.

Personal reading of Scripture should follow this same dynamic. First we listen to the word, take it in as living bread, and digest it into our very being. Then, animated by the living word, we metabolize it into good deeds and devoted witness. The sacred page is transformed through us, in the name of Jesus, into cups of cold water for the thirsty, to feet washed in service, to visits to the imprisoned, to food for hungry children, to compassion for the immigrant and the outcast.

The two disciples on the road to Emmaus recalled their experiences of listening to the Scriptures with Jesus, and they said, "Were not our hearts burning within us while he was opening the Scriptures to us?" As they heard the inspired words, their hearts began to catch fire. In fact, every passage of Scripture is like a burning ember. It has the potential to spark off the page, spread, and consume. And as we read them, we are in danger of catching fire, of letting God's "pentecostal" fire fill our lives.

When our lives are transformed through Scripture, our very being becomes a witness to others.

Most often, when people are asked why they read the Bible, their answers have something to do with information. But Christ, his church, and its liturgy call us to read Scripture for transformation. The faithful reader must become open not only to intelligent understanding of the text but also to personal abduction by its message. When we prayerfully read the great living book of sacred Scripture, we cannot remain the same. The more we remove the obstacles in our way — our impatience, fears, misunderstandings, and complacency — the more powerfully Scripture can burn in our hearts and transform us. Sometimes the changes are remarkable, as we've seen in the lives of the saints. But more often the transformation happens in subtle ways. We can become aware of the fruits of studying the Bible when we discern the fruit of the Spirit within us: "love, joy, peace, patience, kindness, generosity, faithfulness, gentleness, and self-control" (Gal 5:22–23). When we begin to notice this fruit in the way we live each day, we then know that the word of God is transforming us from within.

This personal transformation by the word of God leads believers to become evangelizers. When we read and pray the Scriptures in this way, we cannot help but communicate the good news of Jesus with our lives. When our lives are transformed through Scripture, our very being becomes a witness to others. All of our words and actions communicate to others what animates our lives. The encounter with God in Scripture led the great saints to share their experience with others. St. Paul, St. Augustine, St. Benedict, St. Francis, St. Dominic, St. Ignatius, St. Thérèse, and many others heard the Scriptures as God's living word, and their lives were changed. They joined their lives to Jesus, and they took up the mission of the church, the mission of bringing others to the saving experience of Jesus Christ.

The saints never asked the kinds of questions we ask today of the Bible: Who was the author? What date was it written? Is this or that passage historical or not? What is its literary form? These kinds of questions are important and certainly interesting, but they are not the primary or ultimate questions. The saints ask, rather, what is the truth God wants me to understand? What is God saying to me through these words? How does this passage call me to change? What is God showing me about himself? In what way is this good news for others and myself?

What we notice about many of the books of the Bible, especially the four gospels and the Acts of the Apostles, is that they are open-ended. These works leave their readers with the definite sense that it is up to them to complete the message, to witness to the resurrection, to continue the journey, to continue to witness the good news to the ends of the earth. They convince us that being a disciple of Jesus and a member of his church is not just a static acceptance of Jesus' teachings. It is a dynamic following in Jesus' footsteps, traveling with him along the way, attracting others to this journey, and opening up the horizon of the church to all people.

For Reflection or Discussion

1. What does it mean to say God's word is personal and relational? How does this understanding affect the way you hear and respond to Scripture?

2. What does it mean to trust in the inspiration of Scripture? How do you experience God breathing in the biblical author, within the sacred texts, and within you as you read Scripture?

3. How can you discover your place within the unfolding drama of Scripture? What might God's word be calling you to do as you find your role in God's saving plan for the world?

4. What did St. Augustine mean when he said that the Old Testament is unveiled in the New Testament? How can you learn to see the good news of Jesus Christ on every page of Scripture?

5. How does your appreciation of the Bible develop when you consider it as a work of beauty, as inspired literature that attracts, captivates, and entices?

6. How can eating, chewing, digesting, and assimilating Scripture help you develop a biblical imagination? How does this holistic reading of Scripture help you become a better evangelizer?

7. How does the liturgy of the church enable you to hear the voice of God in Scripture and experience Christ's living presence in the word more readily? How does the Mass lead to evangelization?

Evangelization at the Heart of Sacred Scripture

Chapter 4

Evangelization in Ancient Israel

The Christian call to evangelize begins in the call of Israel to be God's own people. Against the biblical backdrop of God's good creation and the human choice of sin, God calls forth a particular people and makes them his own. Christian believers are united to the Scriptures of ancient Israel through Jesus Christ as we take on this story of God's people and make it our own. By inserting our own lives into the grand narrative of the Old and New Testaments, we unite our lives with God's mission and orient our lives with hopeful confidence toward the future.

According to Paul, the gospel begins in Genesis. There, in Abraham's divine call to go forth from his homeland and to be the bearer of God's mission, God begins a saving history that will extend to the whole world. God promises Abraham descendants as numerous as the stars of the sky, a land of their own, and most significantly, blessings through him for "all the families of the earth" (Gen 12:3). God desires to bless one people so that through them he can in turn bless all peoples. This is the message that Paul describes as the good news preached in advance, "the gospel beforehand" (Gal 3:8), the proclamation that God's overarching will throughout Scripture is to bring blessings to all the nations.

But the narrative of Abraham is preceded in Genesis by an account of how people were created, along with all of God's creatures, as "very good" (Gen 1–2). The family of humanity was made to be bearers of God's image and likeness in the world. This creation account is followed by stories depicting the consequences of human sin in rebellion, rivalry, mistrust, and shame (Gen 3–11).

The stories of Adam and Eve and their offspring result in the violence and corruption that spreads across the earth and leads to the flood. And finally, the account of the tower of Babel shows that our human attempts to build a society result in confusion and alienation. Against this backdrop, the narrative of Abraham begins. Abraham's trusting response to God begins a narrative that shows God's desire for his family — that it embody God's original design for humanity and anticipate the goal toward which God's redemptive purpose is moving.

Christian believers are united to the Scriptures of ancient Israel through Jesus Christ as we take on this story of God's people and make it our own.

Through the Torah, prophets, and psalms, we come to know God and what kinds of blessings he has in mind for the world. All of these Scriptures are oriented toward the future and impelled by hope. Through increasing revelation, manifested by the words and deeds of God among his people, we come to realize that, from the beginning to the end of God's plan, God desires to continually fashion the world, to heal the world when it goes astray, and to call it to ever-greater justice, beauty, goodness, and truth.

From creation to the promised new creation of all things, the Bible invites us to participate in God's mission to restore and redeem the world. With Israel, we have to look backward, forward, and outward. God's people must look backward to the beginning of time, to his original intention for human life. We must also gaze forward to the end of time, to God's goal, a renewed humanity in a restored creation. And, with Israel, we must face outward to the nations, confronting idolatry, seeking justice, and embodying God's will so that all people might come to know and worship the true and living God. Facing outward as God's people, we join in his mission so that all people might experience his saving grace.

God Forms Israel as a People with a Divine Mission

The account of the exodus from Egypt extends the narrative of Abraham's family to the formation of the nation of Israel. Through

God's choice of this particular people, God wishes to unfold the universality of his reign. God's people will be the concrete form and social embodiment of the salvation that he desires for all. Through the history of Israel, God wants to show the other nations the beginnings of the sort of world he intends to bring about through his saving work. So, this particularity of God's people and their history is not only for themselves. Rather, they have been chosen for the sake of God's glory and his mission, and for the sake of others toward whom God's mission is directed.

Through God's choice of this particular people, God wishes to unfold the universality of his reign.

As slaves in Egypt, God's people are living under Pharaoh, caught up in his divine rule and his idolatrous system. When God sees them living in such harsh conditions, he acts to rescue them. God calls Moses to be his instrument with Pharaoh, and Moses demands that the Israelites be freed to worship and serve God. When Pharaoh refuses, God begins to pour out plagues upon Egypt, Pharaoh, and their gods. God delivers his people with signs and wonders so that the Egyptians will know that God is the Lord and so that Israel will be liberated to render their full allegiance to God alone.

Leading his people into the wilderness, God forms a solemn and binding covenant with them. On Mount Sinai, God tells his people why he, the Lord of all nations, has chosen to liberate one nation and bind them to himself in covenant:

> You have seen what I did to the Egyptians, and how I bore you on eagles' wings and brought you to myself. Now therefore, if you obey my voice and keep my covenant, you shall be my treasured possession out of all the peoples. Indeed, the whole earth is mine, but you shall be for me a priestly kingdom and a holy nation. (Ex 19:4–6)

This is the special identity of God's people and the unique role they will play throughout the remainder of the Bible. Even though the whole earth belongs to God, Israel belongs to God in a special sense and has been chosen for a special task. God's choice of Israel is not an end in itself, but is the means to a much greater end.

God has freed his people, brought them into covenant, and dwells with them in order to carry out his redeeming mission in the world.

Israel is chosen to be "a priestly kingdom." What priests are for God's people, Israel is for the world of nations. In the Old Testament, priests are set apart by God to mediate God's presence and blessings to others. Thus, Israel is called to be a tangible indication of God's presence to the surrounding nations and to bring God's blessings to all the other peoples. In addition, Israel is chosen to be "a holy nation." Holiness is the quality of something that has been set apart and consecrated to God's service. So, Israel has been removed from the other nations and dedicated to God's mission for the world. Throughout the remainder of the Torah, God teaches his people how their lives are to be markedly different from those of the peoples around them. Israel must showcase to the world what it means to be a people in covenant with God.

Israel's distinctive formation as a people by God includes not only their liberation from servitude and their covenant with God; their identity also includes God's living presence with them. God's final instructions to his people in the book of Exodus tell them to build a tabernacle that will be his abode with them. God says to Moses, "And have them make me a sanctuary, so that I may dwell among them" (Ex 25:8). The detailed instructions regarding its structure, building materials, and furnishings express the uniqueness of God's dwelling with Israel and the importance of their worship of God. Worshipping God is now central to the identity of God's people; it is both the impetus and the goal of witness.

God has freed his people, brought them into covenant, and dwells with them in order to carry out his redeeming mission in the world. They are made a priestly and holy people for the sake of the nations, but they will not bring God's blessings and saving presence to others through their own strength. God will be among his people, acting in wonderful deeds to make himself known to the peoples of the earth. God first acts *in* his people, then God works *through* his people for the sake of the world. The people of God are able to witness to God only after experiencing the presence of God with them in word and deed. Only after worshipping God, in proclamation and sacrifice, are they able to witness to his steadfast love and covenant fidelity.

From Twelve United Tribes to a People Dispersed among the Nations

The remainder of the Old Testament narrates how Israel lived out its mission to be the bearer of God's blessings to all the families of the earth. As Israel enters into the land, Moses exhorts the people to observe the Torah so that they will have abundant life and so that they will be a witness to the nations around them:

> See, just as the LORD my God has charged me, I now teach you statutes and ordinances for you to observe in the land that you are about to enter and occupy. You must observe them diligently, for this will show your wisdom and discernment to the peoples, who, when they hear all these statutes, will say, "Surely this great nation is a wise and discerning people!" For what other great nation has a god so near to it as the LORD our God is whenever we call to him? And what other great nation has statutes and ordinances as just as this entire law that I am setting before you today? (Deut 4:5–8)

Israel's land is at the crossroads of the nations so that God's people may be seen by the other peoples. Israel will live out its history under the constant surveillance of the ancient world. Moses urges them to be faithful to the covenant and to follow God's decrees. In this way the peoples of the world will see their wisdom and know that God is near to them.

In addition to fidelity to the Torah, another critical task of Israel in their role as witnesses is the responsibility of instructing the next generation. The people are in constant danger of forgetting God's saving deeds and the way of life God set forth for them. Again Moses urges the people to remember and teach their children:

Take care and watch yourselves closely, so as neither to forget the things that your eyes have seen nor to let them slip from your mind all the days of your life; make them known to your children and your children's children — how you once stood before the LORD your God at Horeb, when the LORD said to me, "Assemble the people for me, and I will let them hear my words, so that they may learn to fear me as long as they live on the earth, and may teach their children to do so." (Deut 4:9–10)

An important part of witnessing is teaching the ways of the Lord to the next generation. Without instruction the children of Israel are in danger of falling into the idolatry of the surrounding nations.

By submitting the life of the nation to God's rule, David brings hope for the future to Israel.

Joined together in the land as a loose confederation of tribes, God's people retold their formative story of exodus and sought to maintain their distinct identity among the peoples of the land. Although the last chapter of the book of Joshua narrates Israel's renewal of the covenant with God in their own land, the beginning of the book of Judges tells how the people compromised the covenant through idolatry and failed to pass on the faith to the next generation (Judg 2:10). Rather than stand as witnesses to their relationship with God, the twelve tribes of Israel continually fall into idolatry and become like the other nations. The book of Judges ends with the question of whether or not a monarchy would help Israel fulfill its calling.

The next era of Israel's saga is characterized by kings with royal courts and priests with wondrous temples. The books of Samuel and Kings describe the monarchy in the line of David and the temple in Jerusalem as God's gifts. They support Israel in its calling to be a holy and priestly nation in witness to the surrounding peoples. David provides a model for what a king for Israel should be. He mediates God's rule, since God is Israel's true king. He removes the threat of idolatry by defeating Israel's enemies. He promotes worship and sacrifice in Jerusalem. And he administers the Torah with justice for the poor and weak so that Israel becomes again an exemplar for the surrounding nations.

By submitting the life of the nation to God's rule, David brings hope for the future to Israel. God makes a covenant with the king, promising that one day one of David's descendants would rule over a universal and everlasting kingdom (2 Sam 7:16; Ps 2:7–8). The psalmist prays that the promise made to Abraham would be fulfilled in Israel's future king: "May all nations be blessed in him" (Ps 72:17). Through the reign of this ideal king in the line of David, Israel will fulfill its calling to bring God's blessings to the peoples of all nations.

The Israelites are not the sole beneficiary of God's blessings. Rather, they are the channel of God's blessings for all peoples.

The temple built by Solomon in Jerusalem brings hope that God's glorious presence and Israel's worship will serve as witness to the world. At the dedication of the temple, Solomon prays that God will not only hear the people of Israel when they pray, but also that God will hear foreigners from distant lands who are drawn to the temple to know and serve God (1 Kings 8:41–43). The king prays that when God hears the prayers of the foreigners, "all the peoples of the earth" may know and invoke God's name. Isaiah envisions the day when God's temple in Jerusalem will be a place of worship and sacrifice for people of all nations and will be called "a house of prayer for all peoples" (Isa 56:6–7).

The hymnbook of the temple, the book of Psalms, nourishes the prayer of God's people and highlights Israel's alternative view of living in the world. But at the same time, the psalms remind God's people of their outward calling for the sake of all peoples. Whatever God does for Israel is ultimately for the benefit of the whole world. Psalm 47 encourages the peoples of the world to applaud

God's deeds among Israel because he is the king of the whole earth
and will one day be acknowledged by all:

> Clap your hands, all you peoples;
> > shout to God with loud songs of joy.
> For the LORD, the Most High, is awesome,
> > a great king over all the earth. (Ps 47:1–2)

Psalm 67 asks that God bless his people, not only for their
own sake, but so that God's salvation may be known among all the
nations of the earth.

> May God be gracious to us and bless us
> > and make his face to shine upon us,
> That your way may be known upon the earth,
> > your saving power among all nations.
> Let the peoples praise you, O God;
> > let all the peoples praise you. (Ps 67:1–3)

The Israelites are not the sole beneficiary of God's blessings.
Rather, they are the channel of God's blessings for all peoples.
Through them, God will extend his blessings to all.

The psalms continually orient God's people toward the nations. Numerous psalms urge Israel to sing of God's deeds among
the nations, and many others summon the nations to praise God.
Other psalms promise a future in which the nations will join Israel in worshipping God. Psalm 22 evokes this hopeful scene:

> All the ends of the earth shall remember
> > and turn to the LORD;
> and all the families of the nations
> > shall worship before him. (Ps 22:27)

The temple and its hymnbook draw in God's people to worship, and then it directs them outward to witness to all. In word,
worship, and witness, God's people express their universal vision
and the ultimate goal of God's saving work among them.

The period of Israel's monarchy ended in disaster because of
the repeated failures of God's people to live according to the covenant. First, the ten northern tribes were defeated by the Assyrians

and scattered throughout their realm. A century and a half later, the southern tribes were conquered, the temple in Jerusalem was destroyed, and priests and many people were deported to Babylon. Stripped of their sovereignty as a nation and deprived of their system of worship, the Israelites learned to live as a minority culture in the midst of pagan conquerors. First subjected to the Babylonians, then the Persian Empire, followed by the Greeks and the Romans, they were in danger of losing their identity as God's holy and priestly people.

The biblical writings of Israel's exile speak against two temptations that would cause Israel to lose its divine mission. The first danger is isolation. Withdrawing from the other nations could protect their own beliefs and practices, but they would fail to be the showcase to the other peoples of the world that God expected them to be. The second danger is assimilation. Identifying themselves with the other nations and assimilating their culture would cause Israel to lose its distinctive identity and dilute its covenant with God. To avoid these two dangers, Israel developed structures of leadership, institutions of worship, and its sacred literature to maintain its unique identity and witness among the foreign empires. In the midst of the overwhelming imperial cultures in which the Israelites live, they must bear in mind their unique God-given identity, the covenanted community to which they belong, and the one God of all the nations whom they serve. They must remember their unique calling to be a blessing to the nations and to await the fulfillment of God's purposes with hope.

The Prophets Call God's People to Be Witnesses to the Peoples of the Earth

The prophets challenge the Israelites when they forget their identity, break the covenant, and obscure their witness to the peoples of the earth. When God's people highlight only their own privilege, seek their own security, and take for granted the salvation they receive from God, the prophets admonish them with threats of destruction. And they persuade them to remember their outward-facing mission. In every period of its history, Israel needs its prophets to renew their identity and direct them toward their missionary responsibility to other nations.

The story of Jonah is a cautionary tale in this regard. When the prophet is commissioned to proclaim God's judgment to the people of Nineveh, the hated enemies of Israel, he ran away and jumped into a boat heading in the opposite direction. After God's relentless efforts to bring him to Nineveh, Jonah prophetically declares the city's impending doom. But the entire city repents, from king to beggar, and God mercifully spares the city. Rather than thank God for bestowing the same incredible mercy on Nineveh as he had bestowed on Israel, Jonah bitterly complains. Jonah was doing what he was called to do, what any prophet ought to do, but he was angry because of God's goodness to these foreigners. The story rebukes Israel for their inward-centered attitude and for projecting their own ethnocentric prejudices on God.

From Israel's central position, "in the midst of the earth," God's blessings have extended to Israel's former oppressors, now Israel's international neighbors.

God's universal project is expressed by Isaiah the prophet. God's plan has always been that "the earth will be full of the knowledge of the LORD as the waters cover the sea" (Isa 11:9). The prophet anticipates a future day when the two great superpowers to the north and south, Assyria and Egypt, will be at peace with Israel through their common worship of God:

> On that day Israel will be the third with Egypt and Assyria, a blessing in the midst of the earth, whom the LORD of hosts has blessed, saying, "Blessed be Egypt my people, and Assyria the work of my hands, and Israel my heritage." (Isa 19:24–25)

From Israel's central position, "in the midst of the earth," God's blessings have extended to Israel's former oppressors, now Israel's international neighbors.

"You are my witnesses," God declares to his people in exile. Taken from their land, with their temple destroyed, all they have left is the word of God. Yet, they are called to the task of bearing witness to God in the arena of other nations and other gods.

> You are my witnesses, says the LORD,
>   and my servant whom I have chosen,
> so that you may know and believe me
>   and understand that I am he.
> Before me no god was formed,
>   nor shall there be any after me.
> I, I am the LORD,
>   and besides me there is no savior.
> I declared and saved and proclaimed,
>   when there was no strange god among you;
>   and you are my witnesses, says the LORD. (Isa 43:10–12)

At the heart of being God's "servant" is being God's "witness." Israel must witness in word and deed to the truth about God. This witness is not wielded with coercive imperial power but by the countercultural, gentle nature of the servant — a servant of God and of the world that waits for God.

The word "evangelize," to declare good news, first occurs in the Old Testament in the context of Israel's imminent release from their exile and captivity in Babylon.

The first purpose of Israel's witness is strengthening their own conviction. God's people are called to witness, first, so that they themselves will "know and believe and understand." Before the exile, Israel had refused to acknowledge God or trust in him. Yet now God is summoning his people anew. God is recalling them to their original mission of being his witnesses. And by being witnesses, Israel will themselves learn to recognize God, understand his ways, and hope in him. The task of witnessing to others reinforces the conviction of the witness.

The second purpose of Israel's witness is offering testimony to others. The truths to which Israel is called to witness are, according to Isaiah, threefold: First, God is one, eternal, and transcendent. "No god was formed" either before him or after him.

God was always there; he alone is unformed. Second, God is the only savior. God's saving power is evident in Israel's history and can be counted on for the future. As the only savior, God has been in control of events that led to the exile and is in control of those that would bring it to an end. Third, God holds supreme control of history. In all the saving events of Israel's history, God says, "I declared and saved and proclaimed." As in the exodus, God declared his intentions, then he executed the saving deed, and then he proclaimed his saving action by his word and taught his people that he is faithful to his promises.

These are the great truths about God to which Israel must testify. What could be more important than the identity, power, and sovereignty of the one living God? And how will the peoples of the world come to know their Savior and Lord? "You are my witnesses," says God. God entrusts the greatest truths of the world and of history to the lives of human witnesses.

The word "evangelize," to declare good news, first occurs in the Old Testament in the context of Israel's imminent release from their exile and captivity in Babylon. Isaiah evokes the imagination and hope of his hearers with the image of a single messenger, an evangelizer running with the good news. Speeding across the mountains, he carries the news and announces it to the ruined Jerusalem, proclaiming that God's promises are being fulfilled.

> How beautiful upon the mountains
>> are the feet of the messenger who announces peace,
> who brings good news,
>> who announces salvation,
>> who says to Zion, "Your God reigns."
> Listen! Your sentinels lift up their voices,
>> together they sing for joy;
> for in plain sight they see
>> the return of the LORD to Zion.
> Break forth together into singing,
>> you ruins of Jerusalem;
> for the LORD has comforted his people,
>> he has redeemed Jerusalem.
> The LORD has bared his holy arm

before the eyes of all the nations;
and all the ends of the earth shall see
the salvation of our God. (Isa 52:7–10)

The heart of the evangelizer's message is this: "Your God reigns." He announces that God's reign brings about "peace," which is harmony in all relationships and the fullness of life, and "salvation," which is deliverance from all forms of bondage and oppression.

Isaiah evokes a scene of great joy in which the sentinels on the crumbled wall of Jerusalem and even the ruins themselves form a jubilant chorus. They see beyond the messenger and realize that the Lord himself is returning to the city to live with his people. God "comforts" his people, ending their sorrow and bringing relief from their pain and grief. God also "redeems" his people, accomplishing their release and restoration.

As a showcase people for the nations, Israel will reflect God's holiness.

The good news that God reigns, returns, and redeems will ultimately benefit "all the nations." The good news spreads from the single messenger to "all the ends of the earth." The word of God opens outwardly from a word directed to Israel to a word with universal scope. God's word becomes good news for all people, a promise of salvation to the world.

God chose and formed Israel so that they would be "a light to the nations" (Isa 42:6; 49:6), so that at last "the glory of the LORD shall be revealed, and all people shall see it together" (Isa 40:5). God wanted to fashion a people whose very existence in the world is a living testimony to his rule over the world. Every aspect of Israel's existence — domestic, social, economic, and political — was to reflect God's character. As witnesses to God's reign, God's people must reflect God's care for the world and especially for those who would otherwise be forgotten or trampled upon: specifically, widows, orphans, the poor, the weak, and the strangers in the land. The prophets understood that it is impossible to witness to God's reign without also criticizing the idolatry and injustice that obscure that witness. The prophets denounce the kings, the priesthood, the courts, or the marketplace — whatever systematically thwarts God's reign.

As a showcase people for the nations, Israel will reflect God's holiness. So, Zechariah envisions a day when the bells of the horses will be inscribed with "Holy to the LORD" and when every cooking-pot will be "sacred to the LORD of hosts" (Zech 14:20–21). Every aspect of Israel's communal life will model God's holiness, not because of any quality intrinsic to Israel, but because of its call to reflect God's glory for the world.

When Israel leaves its captivity in Babylon to return to Jerusalem, it is like a new exodus. As in the original exodus from Egypt, God's act of salvation will reveal God to the other nations.

The prophet Ezekiel knows that God will restore Israel after the exile, not for their own sake, but for the sake of God's name among the nations:

> Therefore say to the house of Israel, Thus says the Lord GOD: It is not for your sake, O house of Israel, that I am about to act, but for the sake of my holy name, which you have profaned among the nations to which you came. I will sanctify my great name, which has been profaned among the nations, and which you have profaned among them; and the nations shall know that I am the LORD, says the Lord GOD, when through you I display my holiness before their eyes. (Ezek 36:22–23)

God makes his holiness known among the nations through his actions on behalf of Israel. Yet, the one who saves Israel can also save all who turn to him. To the peoples of every nation throughout the earth, who heed Israel's witness, God issues this invitation:

> Turn to me and be saved,
>   All the ends of the earth!
> For I am God, and there is no other.
>   By myself I have sworn,
>   from my mouth has gone forth in righteousness a word
>   that shall not return:
>   "To me every knee shall bow, every tongue shall swear."
>   (Isa 45:22–23)

The word of God goes forth from the "mouth" of God and does not return; rather, it accomplishes its aim of announcing salvation to "all the ends of the earth."

From Messianic Hope to the Christian Gospel

The promises of God, embedded in Israel's Torah, historical writings, and prophets, kept hope alive for God's people through long centuries under the oppression of the Babylonian, Persian, Greek, and Roman empires. A small flame of hope shone in the darkness and was not overcome by it. God had promised that Israel would be gathered again from all the places it had been scattered and that the people would be renewed with a "new heart" and a "new spirit" (Ezek 36:24–27). And as Israel is called back to its true purpose, the nations will emerge from the earth's darkness and come to the light of Israel's dawning (Isa 60:2–3). God's purposes in and through Israel will be accomplished when the Messiah brings God's kingdom and as the peoples of the world are incorporated into the renewed Israel. God will reign as universal Lord over a worldwide kingdom.

As the Old Testament period ends, Israel has failed in its mission to be a light to the nations. The people were continuously under the subjugation of foreign powers, languishing in the world's darkness. By the time of the Roman occupation, Israel longed for the Messiah, but the people were torn apart by factions — Pharisees, Sadducees, Zealots, and Essenes — each with a differing vision of the coming kingdom and how God will bring it about. Each vision manifested a profound misunderstanding of God's purpose in choosing Israel. They cultivated attitudes of separatism from other peoples and affirmed their own privileges over all other nations. Their history of being exploited manifested itself in bitter hatred for the Gentiles and a desire for vengeance toward the peoples of other nations.

Israel's condition formed a strong contrast to the holy and priestly nation God intended his people to be. The prophetic image of the coming kingdom of God looked nothing like the historical situation in which Israel found itself. By the time of Jesus, Israel was looking forward to a messiah who would crush and destroy its

Gentile enemies. The divided people hoped that God would punish the peoples of the other nations — an expectation far different from God's desire to bring salvation to the ends of the earth.

If God's people are to be a channel of God's blessings for all the peoples, they need a new heart and a new spirit. They need to be incorporated into a renewed covenant, focusing outward toward the nations. The Old Testament points us in the direction of God's purposes, yet it awaits a new intervention of God to fulfill the divine mission for the world.

For Reflection or Discussion

1. Why does Paul say that God's call to Abraham is the first expression of the gospel?

2. Why does God call one people, the children of Abraham, before he calls and blesses all people?

3. What is Israel's role as "a priestly kingdom and a holy nation" in the context of their covenant with God?

4. What can we learn from both the successes and failures of Israel's history about the call to evangelize other people?

5. What can the church learn from Israel about the opposite temptations of isolation and assimilation?

6. What does Israel learn from the prophets about the call to be God's witnesses? How do the prophets serve as a continual warning and encouragement for the church?

7. Why does Israel need a new covenant, a new temple, a new heart, and a new spirit? Why is the flame of hope so essential for God's people?

Chapter 5

Evangelization in the Gospels

As the pages of Scripture turn from Malachi to Matthew, from the Old Testament to the New, we see Israel's flame of hope blaze up from the earth's darkness and prepare the way for the dawn of God's kingdom. All of the expectation of the Old Testament in relationship to God's desire to bring blessings to the nations through Israel will be brought to fruition in the New Testament. The time has come for the promises to Abraham, the covenant with Moses, the hopes of David and Solomon, and the vision of the prophets to move from the imagination of faith to fulfillment in history. Israel's long-awaited Messiah will inaugurate an evangelizing mission that will bring the good news of God's salvation to the ends of the earth.

During the age of Israel, God's people evangelized by being a witness to the peoples around them. They were to be a light to the nations by living in commitment to their covenant relationship with God. Through God's working within the history of his own people, he wanted to show the other nations the beginnings of the salvation he intends to bring to the world. As a holy and priestly nation, Israel was to face outwardly and be a witness to the nations of the one, true God, yet there was no mandate to go out to the nations as missionaries. Rather, the drawing of all the nations to Zion and the salvation of all peoples was understood as something that God would do in the last days.

With the coming of Jesus as Israel's Messiah, God brings the promised restoration of his people and his own kingdom to Israel. Jesus embodies Israel's hopes and brings God's promises to fulfillment. As Jesus restores Israel to its calling, he forms the nucleus of his church. And in so doing, Jesus transformed the missionary vision of God's people into the energetic practice of evangelization.

Israel's long-awaited Messiah will inaugurate an evangelizing mission that will bring the good news of God's salvation to the ends of the earth.

Announcing the Kingdom of God

The heart of the evangelizing message of Jesus is the announcement of God's kingdom. Beginning his ministry in Galilee, Jesus declares, "The time is fulfilled, and the kingdom of God has come near; repent, and believe in the good news" (Mk 1:15). Although Jesus never clearly defines what he means by "kingdom," his hearers know from the ancient Scriptures that it is the restoration of God's reign over all creation. In Jesus, God's kingdom is imminent. Israel's hope has become actuality. Yet, while Jesus teaches that God's kingdom is a present realization as the new age dawns, God's reign is also still in the future, something for which we must long and pray. So, the kingdom of God is already present but has not yet been manifested in its fullness.

The arrival of God's kingdom means that God is dynamically establishing his rule. God is activating his saving power in Jesus through the Holy Spirit. When John the Baptist sends messengers to ask whether Jesus is the Messiah and if God's redeeming power is at work in him, Jesus sends them to report that "the blind receive their sight, the lame walk, the lepers are cleansed, the deaf hear, the dead are raised, and the poor have good news brought to them" (Mt 11:5). Jesus triumphs over the reign of evil in the world, reversing its consequences: physical and mental disease, demonic possession, shame and guilt, food scarcity, self-righteousness, exploitation of the poor, and even the chaotic forces of nature.

What the people of Israel hoped God would do in the last days is now being done in the ministry of Jesus. In him, the last days are irrupting into the present. He offers his followers an imaginative vision of the world that has immediate and material consequences. Jesus accomplished his evangelization not just with words, but with accompanying deeds. In this way, the whole of his life and ministry may be considered a gospel proclamation, the announcement that God reigns over the earth.

Both the rich and the poor must see themselves as children of God and live as inheritors of God's kingdom.

Jesus' evangelization is neither interior nor ethereal. He does not call his listeners to a different or distant world. Nor is his announcement of God's kingdom private or primarily individual. Rather, Jesus invites his hearers into a community of disciples, a new gathering demanding an altered set of allegiances. He invites them to enter God's kingdom, which takes precedence over one's family relationships and national identities. It challenges the status quo regarding the status of the poor, women, and children, and those otherwise excluded like tax collectors, lepers, prostitutes, and Samaritans. It is through this new family of God, embodying the practices and disciplines that manifest God's reign, that God's kingdom is offered to the world.

The evangelization of Jesus calls for repentance and conversion. If his hearers are to receive God's kingdom, they must first learn to see their lives differently, reorder their values, and leave behind their securities. Those who are rich in the things of this world must allow God's reign to subvert their status quo. They cannot have power and comfort at the expense of those who are weak and suffering. "How hard it will be," Jesus warns, "for those who have wealth to enter the kingdom of God!" (Mk 10:23). However, entering the kingdom also means conversion for the poor. They must end any hardened cynicism and fatalism that prevents them from receiving good news. Both the rich and the poor must see themselves as children of God and live as inheritors of God's kingdom.

The gospel narratives of Jesus at table exemplify the new priorities and allegiances of God's reign. Jesus dined with all sorts of folks — religious leaders, public sinners, tax collectors, rich, and poor — all eating together. Every meal seems to be an anticipation of the everlasting banquet of God's kingdom, manifested by abundance for all and the dismantling of seating hierarchies. Around the table everyone matters, no one is dominant or subordinate, and the truly great ones are those who wash the feet of the guests and serve.

Jesus' announcement of the kingdom, then, is the offering of a divine gift. Like scattered seed, it sprouts and grows (Mk 4:27). We cannot force it, manipulate it, earn it, or make it fit our wants; rather, we must "receive the kingdom of God as a little child (Mk 10:15). Its discovery is comparable to the joy one would experience in finding a great treasure or a valuable pearl. Yet, receiving the gift of God's kingdom calls for a radical decision. It requires repentance and faith, giving one's complete allegiance to Jesus as his disciple. All other loyalties, relationships, and obligations must yield to the reign of God present in Jesus.

Israel Gathered for Its Mission to the Nations

The time between the inauguration of God's kingdom and its full manifestation is an age of gathering and mission. As the Old Testament prophets had announced, Israel would be gathered together again as a prelude to its mission of drawing all the nations to God. So Jesus saw his evangelizing task as restoring Israel and recalling God's people to their primary task of being a channel of God's blessings to all nations.

Jesus offers numerous indications that, in time, God's renewed people will bring the gospel, the good news of God's salvation, to all peoples.

So, before all nations would receive God's saving power, Jesus must first gather and renew Israel. He begins by calling Israel to repent, to turn from its failures, and embrace the kingdom of God. Jesus' intention is never to form a new community separate from Israel, but rather to reform Israel. But unlike other renewal movements within Israel at the time, Jesus does not gather God's people simply to receive the coming salvation of the messianic age. Rather, Jesus gathers a people who will also bring that good news to the whole world.

While Jesus affirms the universal extent of God's kingdom, the personal focus of his mission and that of his disciples is the Jews of his day: "I was sent only to the lost sheep of the house of Israel" (Mt 15:24). He desires to gather God's covenanted but scattered people into the fold. Jesus' choice of the twelve, symbolically representing Israel's twelve tribes, expresses the beginning of Israel's restoration. His twelve represent the nucleus and center of growth for Israel reconstituted. So, after Jesus gathers his community and embodies God's reign for them, Jesus sends out these twelve, instructing them with these words: "Go nowhere among the Gentiles, and enter no town of the Samaritans, but go rather to the lost sheep of the house of Israel. As you go, proclaim the good news, 'The kingdom of heaven has come near'" (Mt 10:5–7). Their evangelizing mission, like that of Jesus, is first to announce God's reign to Israel in order to prepare God's people for the new age breaking into the world.

Although the mission of Jesus' earthly life is focused on Israel, the ultimate horizon of his ministry is much wider. He is always oriented to the final goal that people of all nations will come to faith in the God of Israel and join themselves to God's covenant and to God's holy and priestly people. Jesus offers numerous indications that, in time, God's renewed people will bring the gospel, the good news of God's salvation, to all peoples. For example, Jesus' decision to cross to the other side of the Sea of Galilee, from the Jewish area to the Gentile territory, expresses his determination to face outward in his mission. On the other side, Jesus encounters a man possessed by a legion of unclean spirits, and he heals the man, casting the spirits into a herd of swine. Jesus tells the healed man to spread the word about the mighty deeds and mercy the Lord has shown to him (see Mark 5:18–20). Commissioned by Jesus himself, this man becomes the first Gentile evangelizer.

In another account concerning a Gentile, a Roman centurion informs Jesus about his paralyzed servant. Jesus marvels at his faith and says, "Truly I tell you, in no one in Israel have I found such faith. I tell you, many will come from east and west and will eat with Abraham and Isaac and Jacob in the kingdom of heaven" (Mt 8:10–11). The centurion believes that Jesus' saving power can reach across the divide between Jew and Gentile. And Jesus uses the centurion's faith as an opportunity to announce the goal that all peoples will join Israel at the banquet where God will reign.

The prophets imagined God's kingdom as a banquet with rich food and fine wine (Isa 24:6), so Jesus tells a parable about gathering people for a feast (Lk 14:16–24). When the banquet is prepared, the invited guests make excuses and refuse to come. So the master of the house sends his servants to go out to the roads and lanes to gather anyone who accepts the invitation. The parable indicates that the period between the announcement and the full enjoyment of the banquet is the evangelizing ministry of Jesus and his church. Like the mission of Jesus himself, his church must always reach out to the margins, to those who don't presume an invitation to God's kingdom.

With Israel gathered, renewed, and facing outward, Jesus uses the images of the prophets to recall God's people to their missionary calling. Isaiah said that in the days to come all the nations will come to the Lord's mountain, attracted by the light of God's people. Jesus says to his disciples on the mountain, "You are the light of the world" (Mt 5:14). Filled with the good news of salvation, they will shine as lights to the peoples of the world, and attracted by that light, the people of the nations will enter the kingdom of God. A light is not meant to be hidden but to shine before all. God's evangelizing people are a shining light leading the way out of the world's darkness.

Witnesses of a New Creation Formed in the Death and Resurrection of Jesus

The cross and resurrection of Jesus stand at the center of the world's history. In his dying and rising, a new creation has begun. The death of Jesus marks the end of the old — the reign of evil, sin, and death. They are defeated foes that can no longer hold the world in subjection. The resurrection of Jesus means the beginning of the new — the reign of God. The age to come has now arrived, and the powers of God's reign are now at work in the community of believers.

The cross must be planted at the very center of the church's evangelizing mission. Every aspect of God's redeeming mission in

Christ — defeating the powers of evil, removing the guilt of sin, reconciling enemies, destroying the finality of death — leads to the cross. The cross is the necessary cost of the world's salvation.

No words and no image can adequately convey all that God has accomplished in the crucifixion of Jesus.

Some strands of Christian evangelization tend to stress the accomplishments of Christ on the cross only in terms of individual salvation. But a full biblical understanding of the suffering triumph of Christ on the cross goes far beyond a matter of personal guilt and individual forgiveness. The cross is the place where God's kingdom is manifest in what seems to be its defeat. The cross is where Jesus embodies the reign of God most fully. The personal redemption and salvation of every individual is a participation in the universal victory of Christ on the cross. Individuals enter the new creation through repentance, faith, and baptism. They enter the community that Jesus formed to share in the new life of the kingdom. Then they are called to witness to the gospel and be bearers of that life to others.

No words and no image can adequately convey all that God has accomplished in the crucifixion of Jesus. It is too mysterious to be grasped, too big for the human intellect, too expansive to be stated in a single doctrine. Lesslie Newbigin describes several symbols that the church through the ages has used to express the "happening" that God has accomplished through the cross: "Christ the sacrifice offered for our sins, Christ the substitute standing in our place, Christ the ransom paid for our redemption, Christ the conqueror casting out the prince of the world — these and other symbols have been used to point to the heart of the mystery. None can fully express it. It is that happening in which the reign of God is present."[35]

All Christian mission, everything that we do in the name of Jesus, flows from the cross as its source of vitality. The cross is good news for every area of life that has been touched by evil, sin, and

---

35   Lesslie Newbigin, *The Open Secret* (Grand Rapids: Eerdmans Publishing, 1995), p. 50.

darkness. Because of the cross, the gospel is big enough to redeem every part of the world.

Christopher J. H. Wright writes about the cross as the heart of God's mission in the world. "There is no other power," he says, "no other resource, no other name through which we can offer the whole gospel to the whole person and to the whole world than Jesus Christ crucified and risen."

> Ultimately all that will be there in the new, redeemed creation will be there because of the cross. And conversely, all that will not be there (suffering, tears, sin, Satan, sickness, oppression, corruption, decay, and death) will not be there because they have been defeated and destroyed by the cross. That is the length, breadth, height, and depth of God's idea of redemption. It is exceedingly good news. It is the font of all our mission.[36]

The dying and rising of Jesus completes his task of gathering and renewing Israel. Now the reconstituted people of God can be sent to all nations to bear witness to God's kingdom. Freed from the burdens created by universal sin and empowered by the new life of the resurrection, the gathered community of Christ can now be launched into mission.

Jesus Calls His Disciples to Evangelize

When Jesus called his first disciples from their fishing boats, he said, "Follow me and I will make you fish for people" (Mk 1:17), clearly a calling with a missionary focus. Mark's gospel also tells us that Jesus appointed the twelve "to be with him, and to be sent out to proclaim the message" (Mk 3:14). One task leads to another; disciples must be with Jesus to learn from him, and they are then sent out to announce the gospel. This is the same twofold work of disciples in every age: listening to the word of God and evangelizing.

Before his death, Jesus spoke to his disciples about the suffering that lay ahead for them and about how many of their trials

---

36   Christopher J. H. Wright, *The Mission of God* (Downers Grove, IL: InterVarsity Press, 2006), p. 215.

will parallel those of his own passion. Yet, Jesus refers to these trials as "birth pangs," that is, successive waves of distress that ultimately lead to a joy that far surpasses the pain. In this context, Jesus says, "The good news must first be proclaimed to all the nations" (Mk 13:10). This "must" refers to the unrelenting mission of God to make his salvation known to all the people of the world. God's saving plan will not be complete until this evangelizing mission is accomplished. So, somehow by God's grace, the tribulation that Jesus' disciples experience in their mission will be the very means by which they bear witness to Christ and cause the gospel to be spread to all the nations.

The cross and resurrection, standing at the center of the world's history, gives the course of humanity its meaning and direction.

Only after the resurrection, however, can the evangelization of the nations begin. After Jesus has taken away the sin and punishment of Israel and of the whole world, the good news of salvation can go out to all peoples. The cross and resurrection, standing at the center of the world's history, gives the course of humanity its meaning and direction. In this pivotal event, the human situation is radically renewed. In the resurrection of Jesus, he becomes the "firstborn" from the dead, the "first-fruits" of the new creation. The risen Lord is the first experience of something that will one day fill the whole world, and through him, the powers of the age to come flow into the present.

So Jesus, risen and eternally alive, now gives his disciples the great commission. Each of the four gospels concludes with the risen Jesus commissioning his disciples to bring the good news to all nations (Mt 28:16–20; Mk 16:15–18; Lk 24:45–49; Jn 20:21–23). Yet, Jesus does not present this evangelizing mission simply as a command to be obeyed. Rather, it is the result of knowing the good news and is produced by God's own Spirit. This mission to all peoples is the identity of the community Jesus founded. Evangelization is the overflow of the great gift of salvation.

At the end of Matthew's gospel, the evangelist portrays Jesus as the risen Lord who possesses "all authority in heaven and on earth" (Mt 28:18–19). On the basis of this universal dominion, he charges his disciples to invite all the peoples of the world to submit to his lordship. The eleven disciples meeting Christ on the mountain represent Israel gathered and renewed. God's promises throughout the ancient Scriptures, that all nations would be incorporated into the people of God, will now be concretely realized. The Risen One charges the eleven to go out and "make disciples of all nations," to replicate themselves by creating communities of disciples throughout the world. As Jesus has formed the eleven into disciples, so they are to form others as followers of Jesus, modeling their lives on the life and ministry of Jesus himself.

Most scholars agree that Mark ended his gospel at the empty tomb with the pronouncement by the young man in white that the disciples of Jesus will see him in Galilee (Mk 16:8). This challenges all future readers of Mark's gospel to begin listening to the gospel again with the aim of becoming a disciple of the risen Christ. A few decades later, however, dissatisfied with Mark's ending or thinking it had been lost, writers added other endings to the gospel. In Mark's longer ending, the Risen One appears to the eleven in Galilee and commissions them: "Go into all the world and proclaim the good news to the whole creation" (Mk 16:15). Proclaiming the good news is this gospel's distinctive way of describing the mission. This is the same mission Jesus had given his disciples earlier in the gospel, but now the good news is empowered by the resurrection to be announced "to the whole creation."

The work of the church is a continuation of the redeeming mission of Jesus.

While the missionary task of the disciples is described as "making disciples" in Matthew and "proclaiming the good news" in Mark, in Luke's gospel Jesus commissions the disciples to proclaim "repentance and forgiveness of sins" to all the nations (Lk 24:47). This charge of the risen Savior to go to the nations is taken up by Luke in his second volume, the Acts of the Apostles. Luke's writings emphasize that the ability to evangelize is given by the Holy Spirit whom the disciples will receive. The energy of God's Spirit will empower the church to evangelize the world.

In John's gospel, God is the one who sends. John the Baptist was "sent from God" to bear witness to Jesus (Jn 1:6–7). Jesus was "sent" to make the Father known, to do his will, and to complete his work (4:34; 5:23; 6:38). The Holy Spirit will be sent by the Father (15:26) and by Jesus (16:7) to continue the witness of Jesus in the world. And finally, Jesus sends out his disciples with these words: "As the Father has sent me, so I send you" (Jn 20:21).

This gospel makes a clear connection between the mission of Jesus in the world and the mission of his followers. The work of the church is a continuation of the redeeming mission of Jesus. The church can understand its own sending by looking to Jesus as its model and pattern. So, as we read the gospel accounts, Jesus shows us how to bring the faith to others. But we don't do it under our own power; rather, Jesus will send the Holy Spirit. Indeed, immediately after the gospel tells us that Jesus commissioned his disciples, it says, "He breathed on them and said to them, 'Receive the Holy Spirit'" (Jn 20:22). Reminiscent of God's creative act of breathing into his newly formed human being (Gen 2:7), God breathes his own Spirit into his disciples to create his church.

We are called by God's living word in John's gospel to bear witness to Jesus. We must bravely and resolutely testify to him despite the world's opposition.

The fullness of God — Father, Son, and Holy Spirit — is at work in the evangelizing mission of the church. The Father sends the Son, and the Son sends his disciples, and both the Father and the Son send the Holy Spirit to be with God's newly created people as they go forth into the world. The Spirit will be with the disciples, teaching and guiding them, and bearing witness alongside them. Yet, the Spirit will work even more intensely with the disciples than did Jesus during his earthly life. In the words of Jesus, "Very truly I tell you, the one who believes in me will also do the things I do and, in fact, will do greater works than these, because I am going to the Father" (14:12). The Holy Spirit, the Spirit of truth, will remind the disciples on mission of everything that Jesus said to them (14:26). Just as Jesus spoke only what he heard from the Father (7:16; 8:28; 12:49; 14:24; 17:8), the Holy Spirit speaks what he hears from Jesus. In his final discourse to his disciples, Jesus said,

> "When the Spirit of truth comes, he will guide you into all the truth; for he will not speak on his own, but will speak whatever he hears, and he will declare to you the things that are to come. He will glorify me, because he will take what is mine and declare it to you. All that the Father has is mine. For this reason I said that he will take what is mine and declare it to you." (Jn 16:13–15)

Jesus was completely transparent so that the Father's glory would shine through him. Likewise, the Spirit is utterly transparent so that he will glorify only Jesus. Therefore, since the church's mission comes from the Father, through the Son, and in union with the Holy Spirit, God's people must communicate what they have received from the Trinity so as to give God glory.

John's gospel offers us examples of this kind of evangelizing mission. First, the Samaritan woman, who encountered Jesus at the well of her village, believes what she heard and returns to her village to spread the word. She becomes the first evangelizer in John's gospel. Because of her witness, other villagers come to meet Jesus and believe in him (4:39). Second, Mary Magdalene comes to the empty tomb on Easter morning and meets the risen Lord in the garden. After this encounter, Jesus sends her to the other disciples to tell them what she has seen and heard (20:17–18). Like these evangelizers, we are called by God's living word in John's gospel to bear witness to Jesus. We must bravely and resolutely testify to him despite the world's opposition.

For John's gospel, Jesus is the model of our evangelizing mission. The more we read the gospel, the more we understand what it means to be sent by Jesus to continue God's mission in the world. Jesus' own testimony to Nicodemus shows us a pattern for our own mission. Jesus tells him that no one can enter the kingdom of God "without being born from above" (3:3), "without being born of water and Spirit" (3:5). Entering God's reign requires a personal transformation, not a physical rebirth, but a birth from the Holy Spirit. Witness to Jesus leads people, then, to this new creation through faith in Jesus and baptism into his Spirit.

Unlike the gospels of Matthew, Mark, and Luke, which continue to describe the center of Jesus' preaching as the "kingdom of God," the focus of John's gospel is "eternal life." Through faith and baptism we are born into eternal life. As Jesus continues to speak to Nicodemus, he describes the purpose of his own sending: "For God so loved the world that he gave his only Son, so that everyone who believes in him may not perish but may have eternal life" (3:16). Like the kingdom of God, this eternal life is not an existence reserved for the future. This life is already present through living in Christ and will continue forever. This is the life to which Jesus is referring when he says, "I came that they may have life, and have it abundantly" (10:10). This is the quality of supernatural life that makes life worth living forever.

The work of the church is a continuation of the redeeming mission of Jesus. Jesus said of his death and resurrection, "I, when I am lifted up from the earth, will draw all people to myself" (12:32). The work of the glorified Christ continues. As Jesus was sent by the Father, he now sends us. We are sent to incorporate others into God's mission until the purpose of God's sending his Son and the Holy Spirit is completed.

For Reflection or Discussion

1. What kinds of changes are necessary in the lives of those who wish to be a part of God's kingdom?

2. To whom was Jesus' evangelizing directed? Why was it necessary that Israel be gathered and renewed before the gospel could be brought to the world?

3. In what ways does Jesus teach the people of Israel to face outward toward the periphery?

4. In what sense is the cross both the source and the center of the church's evangelizing mission?

5. Why is evangelization the natural overflow of the salvation Jesus brought to the world in his death and resurrection?

6. In what ways is the missionary task that Jesus gives his disciples expressed differently in the endings of the gospels of Matthew, Mark, and Luke?

7. What does John's gospel tell us about the role of the Holy Spirit in the evangelizing mission of the church?

Chapter 6

Evangelization in the Apostolic Church

The ongoing realization of God's plan for the world can be described as the history of salvation. This divine plan has been revealed and actualized through the words and events of the Old and New Testaments. The Scriptures affirm the continuity of God's plan, which was worked out through the history of Israel, of Jesus, and of the church. Jesus is the center of this saving history, uniting the past, present, and future. He is the one who was promised in the Hebrew Scriptures and who brought salvation through his life, death, and resurrection. And it is Jesus who continues to offer salvation to all humanity through his living presence in the church.

God wants all people everywhere to experience the forgiveness and divine life offered through Jesus Christ. The Acts of the Apostles presents this universal will of God by demonstrating the worldwide mission of the church. It narrates the story of the early church, led by the Holy Spirit, living faithfully in service to others and sent to proclaim the gospel through both words and deeds. In Acts, Jesus is not a hero from the past; he is the Lord of the present. Though established in his heavenly abode, Jesus continues to be present to his community on earth, empowering his apostles to act on his behalf to continue the mission he began.[37]

In the programmatic verse of the Acts of the Apostles, Jesus commissions his apostles to be witnesses, first "in Jerusalem,"

---

37   Stephen J. Binz, *Church of the Holy Spirit, Part One: Acts of the Apostles 1–14* (New London, CT: Twenty-Third Publications, 2013), pp. 5–9.

then "in Judea and Samaria," and finally "to the ends of the earth" (Acts 1:8). This opening-out of the gospel message to a continually wider audience forms the structure of the book. The good news of forgiveness and the manifestation of God's Spirit is offered first to the Jews in Jerusalem, but then to "all who are far away, everyone whom the Lord our God calls to him" (2:39).

During his earthly ministry, Jesus brought an experience of God's reign to all kinds of people, including the outcasts and the marginalized. In Acts, we see a further extension of that mission: to widows, centurions, merchants, jailers, philosophers, governors, kings, and sailors. The gospel reaches into the lives of every imaginable kind of person as disciples of Jesus learn that no one is excluded from God's desire to offer the gospel of salvation and life.

Though established in his heavenly abode, Jesus continues to be present to his community on earth, empowering his apostles to act on his behalf to continue the mission he began.

Beyond Jerusalem, the good news is first spread to the Samaritans (8:4–13). Then the message of salvation is offered to an Ethiopian traveling in Judea (8:26–39). It is then brought to the coastal region, to the inhabitants of Lydda, Sharon, and Joppa (9:31–43). The outreach to the Gentiles, the clearest expression of the church's universal mission, begins with Peter's entering the home of Cornelius and the conversion of his household. The Gentile mission is then followed by the mission to the Greeks in Antioch, and then by the long journeys of Paul with his fellow missionaries. The journeys of Paul extend throughout Asia Minor, into Greece, and finally to the capital of the empire in the city of Rome. When Paul travels to Rome, his witness to Christ has truly become universal.

The Holy Spirit Impels the Church to Evangelize

In a homily addressed to the new ecclesial movements on the Feast of Pentecost, Pope Francis said this about the Holy Spirit:

> The Holy Spirit draws us into the mystery of the living God and saves us from the threat of a church which is gnostic and

self-referential, closed in on herself; he impels us to open the doors and go forth to proclaim and bear witness to the good news of the gospel, to communicate the joy of faith, the encounter with Christ. The Holy Spirit is the soul of mission. The events that took place in Jerusalem almost two thousand years ago are not something far removed from us; they are events which affect us and become a lived experience in each of us. The Pentecost of the Upper Room in Jerusalem is the beginning, a beginning which endures. The Holy Spirit is the supreme gift of the risen Christ to his apostles, yet he wants that gift to reach everyone.[38]

In the Acts of the Apostles, it is the Holy Spirit who is the truest apostle — "the one who is sent" by God to empower and guide the church. The narrative traces the way the Spirit of God guided the community of disciples from the beginning of the church throughout the early stages of its growth. This same Holy Spirit continues to direct the church, which had its origin at Pentecost and is now two thousand years old.

Clearly the Holy Spirit is the animating energy of the church's evangelization.

After the age of the old covenant in which God's Spirit was diffused, being bestowed periodically by God to his chosen prophets, priests, and kings, Jesus is uniquely and profusely blessed by the Spirit. This divine Spirit is the agent of God's action in Jesus throughout his life and the dynamism of his ministry. Jesus does not pass on the Spirit until his earthly mission is complete. But following his resurrection and ascension into glory, he bestows his Spirit permanently within his church. Once this community of disciples receives the Spirit, it is able to act as Jesus did. The Spirit that was his alone is now poured out upon them all. At Pentecost, Peter proclaims, "Having received from the Father the promise of the Holy Spirit, [Jesus] has poured out this that you both see and hear"

---

38   Pope Francis, Homily on the Feast of Pentecost, Vatican City, May 19, 2013.

(Acts 2:33). The church will now minister the presence of Jesus as Lord in the world.

The Holy Spirit guides the evangelization of the early church according to God's designs. In what has been called a "triple Pentecost," Acts narrates the gift of the Spirit first to the Jews, then to the Samaritans, and finally to the Gentiles. In the first Pentecost, many Jewish people who have gathered in Jerusalem accept Peter's invitation to repent, be baptized, and receive the Holy Spirit (2:38). As the witness of Jesus' disciples expands to Judea and Samaria, many Samaritans begin accepting the word of God. So the apostles send Peter and John to pray for the Spirit with the Samaritans, and they "laid their hands on them and they received the Holy Spirit" (8:17). The final expansion of the good news to Gentiles begins in the city of Caesarea. When Peter is speaking to the crowd, he proclaims that "God shows no partiality" (10:34) — that people from any nation can experience God's salvation. While he is speaking, "the Holy Spirit fell upon all who heard the word." The Jews who accompanied Peter are amazed that "the gift of the Holy Spirit had been poured out even on the Gentiles" (10:44–45). This third outpouring of God's Spirit indicates that both Jews and Gentiles could be equally endowed with the gift of the Holy Spirit, thus making way for the expansion of the Christian mission to the whole world. Thus, the Holy Spirit guided the church to evangelize, first in Jerusalem, then into Judea and Samaria, and finally to the ends of the earth (1:8), driving the church to cross every barrier in proclaiming the gospel.

Clearly the Holy Spirit is the animating energy of the church's evangelization. From the time of Pentecost, all the major characters in Acts are empowered by the divine Spirit to speak and act with wisdom and courage. Peter is filled with the Spirit and thus proclaims the message of salvation to the Sanhedrin who have put him on trial (4:8). When Peter and John are released from prison, the entire community of believers "were all filled with the Holy Spirit and spoke the word of God with boldness" (4:31). The seven selected to assist the work of the apostles are "full of the Spirit and of wisdom" (6:3). And Stephen, in particular, is "full of faith and the Holy Spirit" as he witnesses even to his death (6:5; 7:55). Philip is guided by God's Spirit to join the Ethiopian in his chariot, to proclaim the good news to him, to lead him to baptism, and then to evangelize all the towns in the region (8:29, 39). Saul, also called Paul, receives the Holy Spirit at his initial experience of conversion (9:17), and the Spirit continues to guide his mission throughout the world. Barnabas and Saul are "sent out by the Holy Spirit" to new lands (13:4). On Paul's final and fateful journey to Jerusalem, the Holy Spirit both warns him of suffering and compels him to go (20:22–23). Nothing can stand in the way of God's plan that Paul will evangelize in the power of the Holy Spirit to the ends of the earth. By demonstrating how all the major figures of the early church are animated by the Holy Spirit, the book of Acts shows us that the whole church is guided and energized by the Spirit to be God's evangelizing people.

This testimony of Acts about the work of God's Spirit within the church presents a number of conclusions for understanding the role of the Holy Spirit in the church today: 1) The Holy Spirit is the origin and source of life for God's church. 2) We are filled with the Holy Spirit through faith and baptism. 3) As disciples filled with the Holy Spirit, we carry on the work of Jesus in our era. 4) The Holy Spirit empowers us to speak boldly and to act courageously. 5) Because the Holy Spirit fills the lives of believers, Jesus can be present to more people and do more than the limitations of his earthly life allowed. 6) The Holy Spirit guides the church in its mission of evangelization. 7) The mission of the church is universal, crossing every barrier to extend to all people. 8) The Holy Spirit leads us individually to seek out people who are ready for a deeper experience of faith. 9) The Holy Spirit guides the leaders of the church to make decisions that conform to God's will. 10) The Holy Spirit compels us to go places and do things that involve risk and suffering.[39]

The Mission of Peter and Paul

Peter and Paul are the two indispensible pillars of the church. These men could not have been more different: Peter was a fisherman from Galilee and Paul a Greek-educated intellectual. But

39   Stephen J. Binz, *Church of the Holy Spirit, Part Two: Acts of the Apostles 15–28* (New London, CT: Twenty-Third Publications, 2013), pp. 3–5.

Jesus brought them together to build his church. The New Testament presents each of their lives as an inspiration and guide for the church's evangelization through the ages.

Despite the distinctive role of Peter among the disciples, he seems to be a mass of contradictions.

Peter is the most prominent of Jesus' disciples, appearing in the gospels more frequently that all the others combined. He is the first called by Jesus and made a fisher of men and women, and he is often the spokesperson for the other disciples. He is the first to profess genuine faith in Jesus, and he is named first by Paul as witness to Jesus' resurrection. In the life of the early church, Peter is shown to exercise a clear primacy. He preaches the first sermon at Pentecost, converting thousands to belief in Christ; he performs the first recorded miracle in the apostolic church, healing a crippled beggar in the name of Christ; and he is the first to convert a Gentile, opening the mission of the church to all people.

Yet, despite the distinctive role of Peter among the disciples, he seems to be a mass of contradictions. He confesses that Jesus is the Son of God, then refuses to accept Jesus' mission as the suffering Messiah. Jesus appoints him as the rock foundation of his church, but Peter shows himself a stumbling block on Jesus' path to the cross. He bravely walks on the water at the direction of Jesus, but then fearfully begins to sink like a stone. Peter reverently offers to erect tents on the mountain when Jesus appears in glory but falls asleep when Jesus asks him to watch with him in his grief. He promises to lay down his life for Jesus but that same night denies three times that he ever knew him. Peter displays a wide range of responses, from his foolish bluster to passionate commitment to Jesus. Peter the disciple weeps in anguish after denying his master, but this same deliriously happy fisherman jumps into the water and swims at breakneck speed to meet his risen Lord. In the early days of the church, he risked his reputation to share the gospel with Gentiles, but later refused to eat with them in Antioch and is reprimanded by Paul. Peter is bold and cowardly, impulsive and fearful, filled with bravado, yet weak, flawed, and sinful.

Though Peter fails often to live up to his calling, through his humility and repentance he grows in his discipleship. He never tried to minimize, justify, or rationalize his own mistakes but honestly confesses his sins. The biblical writers show us that Peter's own accomplishments do not create his heroic character; rather, he is defined in Christian history by what the love of Jesus has wrought in him. Peter challenges us to confront the truth of our own brokenness, so that God's grace can fashion us into the disciples Jesus calls us to be.

Paul's multicultural background made him just the right candidate to bring the gospel to all the nations.

Two primary images identify Peter as an evangelizer. The first is Peter as fisherman. Although casting nets to bring in fish was the trade that Peter knew, Jesus invites him to leave his fishing boat to follow him, becoming a fisher of people. As he had lured fish into his nets, he now attracts men and women, inviting them into the great net of salvation through the evangelizing work of the church. As a missionary, Peter proclaims the gospel to the Jews of Jerusalem and the surrounding areas and initiates the outreach to the Gentiles. The second image is Peter as shepherd of the church. By supervising Christian communities, guarding God's flock, warding off dangers, and leading the fold with care, Peter fulfills the task of tending the sheep left to him by the risen Lord. Following the example of Jesus, the Good Shepherd, Peter pastors the flock of Jewish Christians and reaches out to offer the pasture of salvation to all. Like his master who laid down his life for his sheep, Peter gives his life for the church, beginning in Jerusalem and ending with his martyrdom in Rome.[40]

Paul's influence on the growth and development of the Christian faith was enormous. Although he was a persecutor of Christian believers and seemed an unlikely candidate for the work of evangelization, Paul's multicultural background made him just the right candidate to bring the gospel to all the nations. First of all,

---

40   Stephen J. Binz, *Peter: Fisherman and Shepherd of the Church* (Grand Rapids: Brazos Press, 2011), pp. 1–5.

as a Jew, Paul was loyal to the Torah and awaited the coming of God's kingdom as foretold by the prophets. He always remained a proud member of this ancient faith and understood his mission within the context of its sacred Scriptures. Secondly, as a Greek, Paul not only spoke Greek in addition to Hebrew and Aramaic, he was also immersed in Hellenistic culture. Because he was a native of Tarsus, a center of Greek learning, Greek literature, philosophy, and rhetoric enriched his viewpoint. And because he read the Bible in Greek, the Septuagint version of the Scriptures of Israel, he was able to explain the texts in the language of his audience. Thirdly, as a Roman, Paul used the privileges of his citizenship to his advantage. He used the massive system of Roman roads and commerce to travel thousands of miles establishing churches in cities throughout the Roman world. Yet, Paul was not an uncritical inhabitant of the empire of Caesar. The cult of emperor-worship and the massive power of the empire to crush those who tried to interfere with its absolute authority were strong contrasts to the way of Christ that Paul discovered. In the face of the imperial propaganda that proclaimed Caesar as savior and lord, Paul preached the defiant and subversive gospel message that Jesus Christ is the Lord of the world and the Savior of all.

Paul described himself as a man who had become "all things to all people" (1 Cor 9:22). He used his wide experience and breadth of thought for the sake of the universal gospel he proclaimed. Paul was a man who could talk with rabbis on the streets of Jerusalem and with philosophers on the streets of Athens. He felt at home in the world. He knew the ancient wisdom of the Hebrew Scriptures, and he knew the wisdom of Greek literature, like Homer, Sophocles, and Plato. He possessed a Jewish name, Saul, and a Greek and Roman name, Paul.

Evangelization for Paul meant proclaiming a gospel that was expressed through the Scriptures and symbols of Israel (the Torah and the temple), through the language and worldwide thought patterns of Greece (philosophy and rhetoric), using the communication and transportation systems of Rome to his advantage. He traveled up to the temple in Jerusalem for the feasts of Israel, and he journeyed along the Roman roads out to all parts of the world. He knew that the God of Israel was the Creator and Sustainer of the whole world, and therefore, he became a man of the whole world in order to bring the very Jewish message of the gospel to all people.[41]

The church must always move out into the world, and at the same time, it must always draw people in.

Peter and Paul, so unlike one another and so unlikely to become the great evangelizers they are now known to be, providentially worked together to witness to Jesus Christ and build up his church. Peter journeyed from the weakness of denial to be the rock of fidelity; Paul moved from the blindness of persecution to the fire of proclamation. The narrative of the early church found in the book of Acts focuses its first part on Peter (Acts 1–12) and its second part on Paul (Acts 13–28). Paul envisioned the church's mission field divided between Peter, sent by the Lord to the circumcised Jews, and himself, sent to the uncircumcised Gentiles (Gal 2:7–8). Christ used the parallel ministries of Peter and Paul as an ongoing sign of his church in which the entire spectrum of humanity would find their place in God's reign.

Peter and Paul seem to express two critical aspects of evangelization. To use a metaphor from physics, Peter represents the centripetal force, moving in a curved path inwardly toward the center, and Paul represents the centrifugal force, moving outwardly away from the center. On the one hand, Peter worked to preserve the unity of the church, holding together the opposing positions of James and Paul, and expressing the rock-hard foundation of the community. Paul, on the other hand, moved outwardly to spread the gospel to the whole world. He was a boundary breaker, pushing the church to the fringes, always seeking to remove the barriers that divided people from one another and from God. Both aspects of evangelization, represented by Peter and Paul, are essential for witnessing God's kingdom in the world. Without the unifying force of Peter, Paul's mission would become scattered and would be forever in danger of dissolution. And without the energy of Paul, Peter's mission would become stagnant, and the church would always

---

41   Stephen J. Binz, *Paul: Apostle to All the Nations* (Grand Rapids: Brazos Press, 2011), pp. 1–4.

remain in its status quo. The church must always move out into the world, and at the same time, it must always draw people in.

Evangelization in the Letters of the New Testament

Fortunately for us, Paul not only traveled and preached the gospel, he also wrote letters. The first thirteen letters of the New Testament were written by Paul and his close associates. In them we find a man of passionate zeal and deep love for Christ and the people of his churches. Paul was not only the church's greatest missionary, he was also its first theologian. In his letters we find much about Paul's understanding of Jesus Christ and why his gospel must be brought to the world.

All thirteen of the Pauline letters contain his characteristic greeting, "grace and peace to you." This is a remarkable combination of a Greek salutation, grace (*charis*), which seems to summarize the gospel in a single word, and the ancient Hebrew blessing, peace (*shalom*), which expresses the fullness of well-being that God desires for his people. In this unique greeting, Paul addresses Gentile and Jewish believers together, as members of one church.

**Through their unity, exemplary conduct,
mutual love, and radiant joy, Christians evangelize
by being who they are in Christ.**

Notice that Paul did not write, "*Charis* to you Greeks and *shalom* to you Hebrews." Grace is not just for Gentiles and peace is not just for Jews. God desires the whole body of Christ to receive his grace and to experience his peace. Writing to communities that were often divided and torn by factional strife, Paul addressed them with respect for his readers' own ethnic and cultural backgrounds, yet he also reminded them that they were called to be a new countercultural reality. The church is not a congregation created by simply linking Jews and Gentiles together, but a unified body of Christ, an evangelized people made new in the risen Lord.

The heart of Paul's teaching is the individual and communal experience of union with Christ. We live in Christ; Christ lives in us. We are united with Christ through faith in his saving death and resurrection. Crucified with Christ in baptism, the old self dies, and risen with Christ in baptism, we live a new life. This new life involves a new way of seeing, a new way of being, a new way of living — indeed a new identity. To be "in Christ" means to live as a "new creation" (2 Cor 5:17).

As a new creation "in Christ," we are incorporated into the saving community, the body of Christ. This is a community in which the boundaries that divided people between Jews and Gentiles, slaves and free people, rich and poor, women and men, are transcended. Paul envisions a church that not only includes all of these but also brings them into interdependent relationships. Life in Christ is liberated life. A believer is no longer imprisoned by the prejudices, resentments, and jealousies that so often dominate human life. Part of the dramatic witness the church offered to first-century society was this attractive, alternative community of dissimilar people called into a higher unity in Christ. When we extend grace to others and make peace with one another, we become boundary breakers, and, in so doing, we offer a powerful witness of Christ to our world.

The church, when it embodies the life of God's new creation, is attractive to the world. Its primary mission is to be the living sign of God's redeemed creation for the sake of his glory. Through their conduct, believers either attract others or put them off. When the church is attractive, people are drawn to it, even when the church is not actively going out on mission. Paul tells the young churches that their new life must be evident to all, that they must win the respect of outsiders and shine as stars in the midst of the corrupt and perverse culture of the Roman Empire. Through their unity, exemplary conduct, mutual love, and radiant joy, Christians evangelize by being who they are in Christ.

Paul, more than any other, was responsible for the transformation of a messianic movement within Judaism into the global church. Yet, his turn to the Gentiles and his evangelization throughout the Roman Empire were not just the result of a slow response among his fellow Jews. Rather, Paul understood that his mission to the nations was rooted in God's ancient revelation to Israel. As a result of his experience of the risen Lord, Paul began to interpret and understand the Jewish Scriptures in the light of

Christ's coming. He was convinced that Jesus died on the cross so that in him "the blessing of Abraham might come to the Gentiles" (Gal 3:14). He realized that the prophets and sages of Israel taught that while God sustains a special relationship with Israel, his rule extends to the entire universe. According to these Scriptures, God's Servant would play a decisive role in bringing God's salvation to all people: "I will give you as a light to the nations, that my salvation may reach to the end of the earth" (Isa 49:6). Paul saw that God's ancient desire to bring salvation to the nations was being fulfilled through Jesus, God's Servant and Messiah.

**The gospel is not a slickly packaged self-help scheme competing for attention with other popular ideas.
It is the announcement of God's shocking intervention to save and transform the world.**

The church must always look backward to its starting point in Judaism, to God's gift of the crucified and risen Messiah, who enables people to share in the life of God's kingdom. But it must also look forward toward the unbelieving world, which has yet to know the salvation accomplished in Jesus Christ. The church is the link between the gospel and the doubting, skeptical world. In word and sacrament, Christ is made present to the community of his church. And in turn, this community is called to be the means by which Christ is made present to the world.

Paul gives us insights into his motives and methods for evangelization throughout his letters. In writing to the Corinthians, he clarifies his calling from Christ "to proclaim the gospel" of the saving cross of Christ:

> For Christ did not send me to baptize but to proclaim the gospel, and not with eloquent wisdom, so that the cross of Christ might not be emptied of its power. For the message about the cross is foolishness to those who are perishing, but to us who are being saved it is the power of God. (1 Cor 1:17–18)

The essence of the gospel, Paul explains, is God's saving work through the cross of Christ. It is a message that cannot be delivered with smooth and eloquent rhetoric because salvation through the rugged and torturous cross is an outrageous defiance of worldly expectations. The substance of the message determines the appropriate style of its presentation. The gospel is not a slickly packaged self-help scheme competing for attention with other popular ideas. It is the announcement of God's shocking intervention to save and transform the world.

Although the cross expresses weakness, humiliation, and defeat in the logic of human wisdom, its meaning is transformed by the God who topples the wisdom of the world. In the eyes of the shrewd, the cross seems embarrassing and tragic, but its significance is upended by the one who was stretched out upon it. For those called by God, this mind-boggling paradox of the crucified Savior is the power and the wisdom of God. Here is truth that cannot be argued with reason or imposed with power. It has to be revealed by God, which is the reason Paul received his call to proclaim the gospel of the cross to an incredulous world longing for salvation.

Paul knows that all boasting and self-assertion are incompatible with the evangelization to which he is called. "If I proclaim the gospel, this gives me no ground for boasting, for an obligation is laid on me, and woe to me if I do not proclaim the gospel," Paul declares (1 Cor 9:16). He knows that his ministry is not something that he has merited or earned; rather, it originated as a gift of God's mercy. For this reason, Paul rejects any cunning or deceptive practices in proclaiming the gospel. Called and commissioned by God, he evangelizes in openness and honesty, refusing to compromise the truth and beauty of the gospel he has received.

The evangelizing community that Peter envisions is both at odds with its cultural setting and engaged with it.

Everyone experiences their own poverty and weakness in bringing to the world the precious treasure of the gospel. As Paul reminds us, "We have this treasure in clay jars, so that it may be made clear that this extraordinary power belongs to God and does not come from us" (2 Cor 4:7). This must always give us courage, knowing that the power of evangelization comes from God and belongs to him. We are earthen vessels containing the priceless gift of the gospel. Our mission is not optional, but essential to who we are as baptized followers of Jesus Christ. We are humble instruments of God's mercy, his tenderness, his love for every man and every woman.

The letters of Peter, like those of Paul, reveal a man of passionate zeal for Christ and his church. He teaches his listeners how to live the Christian life in the midst of a world that is not oriented toward its Creator. In his first letter, Peter addresses his readers as "the exiles of the Dispersion" (1 Pet 1:1). Drawing on the Old Testament imagery of the exile and scattering of God's people, he exhorts believers to live as strangers and aliens in a foreign and sometimes hostile environment. The challenge is to be *in* the culture of the world but not *of* it. They are a people who have received "a new birth into a living hope through the resurrection of Jesus Christ from the dead" (1 Pet 1:3). As a newly created people, they live an alternative life with an alternative focus in the midst of the political, social, and cultural institutions of the larger society.

The evangelizing community that Peter envisions is both at odds with its cultural setting and engaged with it. Although the church is a stranger to many aspects of the Roman culture in which it lives, it does not withdraw into a ghetto but involves itself with the existing cultural institutions. While opposing the idolatrous ways of the empire, Christians should accept the authority of human institutions and conduct themselves well in public life so that the unbelievers will "see your honorable deeds and glorify God" (1 Pet 2:12).

Peter offers the imagery of Israel's temple and priesthood: "Like living stones, let yourselves be built into a spiritual house, to be a holy priesthood, to offer spiritual sacrifices acceptable to God through Jesus Christ" (1 Pet 2:5). Jesus spoke of his body as the new temple raised up by God. The building of this new temple has begun in the resurrection. This new temple of God's presence is established in the midst of the nations. It is a people who are given the new life of Christ's resurrection as they are filled with the Holy Spirit. This holy temple exists for the purpose of worshipping God. In contrast to the temple of ancient Israel, made of hardened stones, this spiritual house is made of "living stones." Rather than an inherited priesthood made only of the family of Levi, all Christians form a "holy priesthood." Instead of material sacrifices, Christians offer "spiritual sacrifices" of prayer and praise, of self-consecration and self-giving. Such sacrifices are acceptable to God not on account of the one offering them but because they are made "through Jesus Christ," that is, joined with his perfect sacrifice and united with his Spirit.

To this wonderful image of the church as God's new temple, Peter adds more: "You are a chosen race, a royal priesthood, a holy nation, God's own people, in order that you may proclaim the mighty acts of him who called you out of darkness into his marvelous light" (1 Pet 2:9). These images, derived from Israel's experience of the exodus (Ex 19:5–6), show that the church is the heir to the promises God made to his people of old. In applying these sacred titles to the church, Peter recognizes that God's saving plan is continued and fulfilled through the community of Christian believers. The church is chosen, like Israel, to proclaim God's mighty acts. God's people must witness to Jesus Christ, to his cross and resurrection. It is a priesthood chosen to mediate God's salvation in a darkened world. It is a holy people set apart from the world in order to serve the world. As God's people the followers of the Lord must evangelize in word and deed to a world longing for the light of truth, goodness, and beauty manifested in Jesus Christ.

When the people of the world see the church at its best, they begin to ask questions. When they see how Christians trust in God despite frustration and setbacks, they want to know why. When they see believers love one another and even the seemingly most unlovable, they want to know the reason. When they see people filled with joy that is constant despite suffering and setbacks, they want to know the source of such joy. Peter says to his listeners, "Always be ready to make your defense to anyone who asks from you a reason for the hope that is in you. Yet do it with gentleness and reverence" (1 Pet 3:15–16). When people ask such questions, we must be ready to respectfully give them the answer. We cannot keep to ourselves the word we have heard, the gospel we have received, the hope that is within us.

For Reflection or Discussion

1. In what sense is the Acts of the Apostles all about evangelization?

2. How does Acts show that the Holy Spirit is the animating power of the evangelizing church?

3. How do you experience the work of the Holy Spirit in your own evangelizing mission?

4. In what ways could Peter be a model for you in living out your mission as a disciple of Jesus?

5. How can your understanding of different cultures, languages, and wisdom of the world make you a better messenger of the gospel to others?

6. In what ways do Peter and Paul represent opposite but complementary aspects of evangelization?

7. How is the church to be a living sign to the world, according to Paul's writings? In what ways does the church evangelize the world?

Evangelizing the Church and the World through Sacred Scripture

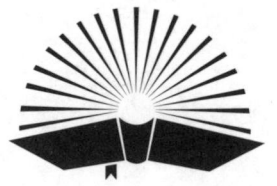

Chapter 7

Becoming Communities of the Word

We have looked at Scripture, the history of the church, and the lives of the saints to demonstrate how listening to the word of God leads to witnessing to the word of God. So, in the church today, we must explore how to become communities of the word, people who allow ourselves to be formed by the inspired Scriptures, because the church cannot bring God's word to others unless we ourselves know and live that word. We cannot evangelize to the world unless we have first been evangelized from within.

The purpose of the church is to be a luminous witness of the word of God to the world. If we want the church that Jesus founded to truly evangelize, then the Scriptures must be at its heart. The Bible must be heard, pondered, and prayed by believers within a community enlivened by God's Spirit. Parishes and movements within the church must become communities of the word in order to be communities that bring the good news of Jesus Christ to the world.

Catholic Bible Study for the Third Millennium

After three decades of work in the field of Catholic Bible study, I have seen what happens when the lives of Catholics are renewed through the study of Scripture. In the last decades of the twentieth century, Catholics came a long way toward becoming a people explicitly shaped by Scripture. In the twenty-first century we must redouble our efforts, building on what we have learned, and continue working to be a people formed by God's word.

When people discover the riches of Scripture together, encourage one another, and share the insights they receive, this is a wonderful way to grow in love for the word of God.

With the encouragement of the teachings of the church, Catholics after the Second Vatican Council experienced a deep hunger for Scripture. A rich fare of biblical texts was laid out in the new Lectionary, and priests and deacons were encouraged to offer biblically based homilies. Dioceses expanded their catechetical ministries to include adult formation, and Bible study became an important offering. Parishes began to sponsor Bible study programs, and Catholics got to know the Bible and began to study and discuss its books. Since the primary way of studying Scripture in the twentieth century was the historical-critical method, this methodology was reflected also in popular studies. This scholarly way of studying the Bible is concerned with the history of the text, its literary forms, its cultural background, and the meaning intended by its original human author. This way of Bible study helped Catholics avoid an overly subjective interpretation and moved the church from a devotional approach to Scripture to a more objective study.

As we discern what the church needs in the twenty-first century, we must be careful not to lose the ongoing discoveries provided by the historical-critical method. We must continue to learn the contexts and literary forms of biblical texts and how to seek the objective meaning intended by the author. But we must add other dimensions to that pursuit by retrieving ancient methods of formation in Scripture, especially the wisdom of lectio divina. So the best form of Bible study today includes commentaries that offer the best in scholarship but also teach us how to reflect individually and with the church on the biblical texts. We must learn how to listen personally to the texts and how to seek a prayerful, contemplative understanding and love for Scripture.

Back in the twentieth century the primary way of engaging in Bible study was forming small groups to meet once a week for shared learning and discussion. This experience of small communities gathered around God's word is a model that continues to be used effectively throughout the world. When people discover the riches of Scripture together, encourage one another, and share the insights they receive, this is a wonderful way to grow in love for the word of God.

So, again, as we discern what we need in our century, let's not neglect the experiences people gain in small faith communities. We must develop these methods so that these groups become more abundant in parishes today. But forming small groups cannot be the only way that people are led to develop the practice of Bible study. If we have thirty people coming to a weekly Bible study and there are three thousand in our parish, we are helping one percent. Any good shepherd would be concerned about the other ninety-nine percent.

We've got to be more creative, more expansive, bringing the whole community to an encounter with Scripture. If we did not restrict parish Bible study only to those people who are able or who desire to meet each week with a small group, we could envision lots of creative ways to bring more people into the experience of studying the Bible. Since most Bible study programs are designed to be used by people working either on their own or in the context of a small group, take advantage of this flexibility to offer Bible study for the whole parish. When adopting a Bible study, form small groups, offering convenient options for people in different circumstances. But never forget to offer the program to those who choose to study the Bible on their own, whenever they can grab ten minutes in their busy day. Take orders for study books at the Sunday Mass to get as many people involved as possible.

A twenty-first-century blend of individual study and work in a small group is the online group using social media. Individuals read and reflect separately, then post their insights online and respond to the thoughts of others. Individuals can reflect and post on their own schedule, yet still experience some of the same advantages of an intimate group. We've got to be creative today in thinking of ways to invite everyone into a regular engagement with Scripture.

Whether members are following a Bible study on their own or with a small group, the faith community is listening together to the same texts. The whole parish is forming the habit of daily Bible reading and reflection. And reflecting on the same text, the whole community is learning to read the Bible for their ongoing growth in Christ and personal transformation in him. The results in a parish can be incredible as a critical mass of parishioners begin to engage with Scripture together and learn how to be more effective witnesses to the word.

Back in the twentieth century, Catholics had a lot of catching up to do, and we studied Scripture primarily either for information or apologetics. We wanted to increase our knowledge and understanding of the Bible, or we wanted to learn how to defend our faith and learn how the Bible was the foundation of the church's doctrine. Again, these motives are noble and should certainly not be discarded today.

But in the twenty-first century, we must study Scripture in a way that leads to the New Evangelization. That means that first we seek to be evangelized ourselves by God's word. Listening to Scripture, seeking to understand its message, reflecting on the texts, and praying in response to Scripture naturally changes us. And, as our lives become more deeply rooted in Christ, we become more effective witnesses to his presence in the world. We gradually become evangelizers of others when our lives are nourished on the word of the Lord.

Taking Away the Obstacles to Growth

A seed is an amazing thing. It looks small and nondescript, yet in the seed is the whole plant, the stalk and its leaves, the fruit-bearing vine. The seed doesn't look like the plant, but given the right environment, it inevitably grows into what it was made to be. There is potency and incredible potential in the seed.

Jesus knew the power of the seed from sowing fields in Galilee. So in his parable of the sower, Jesus says, "The sower sows the word" (Mk 4:14). The sower of the seed doesn't cast the seed only in those places where he knows the soil is just right. He casts it far and wide. Some of the seed falls on the path, and the birds immediately come and eat it up. The seed never even begins to grow. Some falls on rocky ground, so it starts growing quickly, but it soon withers because it can't grow roots. Some falls among thorns, so it begins growing, but after a while it is choked by the weeds and is unable to bear fruit. And some seed falls on good soil, where it bears a harvest of thirtyfold, sixtyfold, and a hundredfold. Yet, even on good soil, where it bears fruit plentifully, the seed's fruit-bearing abundance depends on how well it is cared for, how competently it is plowed and pruned, and how attentively it is fertilized and watered.

The Bible was indeed written long ago, but it is relevant today because it deals with the most basic questions of our humanity.

Over my years of teaching the Bible to diverse audiences, I've often asked people to describe the obstacles that stand in the way of their engagement with Scripture. Listening to their honest replies has led me to continually try to develop resources for Bible exploration and reflection. Here are some of their responses: "The Bible just seems to be too big and overwhelming to tackle it"; "I find it hard to believe that I will understand much of the Bible because even scholars argue over its meaning"; "The Bible doesn't seem to be relevant to life today because it is written in ancient languages about events that happened so long ago"; "It seems like people can interpret the Bible however they wish and it's a constant source of controversy and division among people"; "I've had too many legalistic experiences of people trying to rule my life with the Bible"; "I just don't experience the Bible as a place where God speaks to me"; "I've been doing fine without reading the Bible so I don't see why I should start now."

These statements represent some of the obstacles that prevent the seed of God's word from growing and bearing fruit. These are the kinds of concerns that most people honestly face when they consider the possibilities of regular engagement with the Bible. It is these kinds of uncertainties that sometimes prevent people from ever beginning to really hear Scripture as a disciple of Jesus. Let me try to respond to some of these obstacles that block the seed from putting down roots, shooting upward toward the sun, and bearing flowers and fruit.

First of all, the ideal way to read the Bible is not from cover to cover. The Bible is a small library of books, and each book is different and unique. Good Bible study books can help readers choose a particular book or theme to read and reflect upon. By focusing on small pieces of the Bible, the task ahead feels less intimidating. Second, the Bible was never meant to be difficult. It was written mostly by simple people, like fishermen, tentmakers, and shepherds. The biblical books were written about human experiences that show God's presence and guidance, and they were never intended to contain any mysterious language. While parts of the Bible might seem difficult to understand at first, Bible studies contain commentaries to help readers interpret the meaning of challenging passages. Third, the Bible was indeed written long ago, but it is relevant today because it deals with the most basic questions of our humanity. The essential needs and longings of human beings who reach out to God are the same for all people in every time and place. The questions and struggles of our modern human existence are essentially the same as those of the people of the Bible.

A fully renewed and evangelized church can only come about when Catholics learn to encounter Christ through sacred Scripture and let the Holy Spirit move us to witness.

Fourth, the Bible was never intended to cause conflict between people. Using the Bible to prove points or win arguments is an abuse of the Bible. The Bible is our sacred literature, and we must approach it with humility and wonder. We can leave the controversies to the scholars to hash out. Fifth, some distorted presentations of the Bible do indeed present it as a book of laws and regulations, intended to impose caution and fear. But the Bible is not intended to condemn or confine us. Rather, its purpose is to captivate us. Sixth, when we read the Bible as an insider rather than an outsider, we slowly discover that the Bible is the privileged place where we experience the communication of God with us. If we seem to be getting along fine without reading the Bible, realize that Scripture has offered a deep experience of God's presence to countless people through the ages.

When we remove these obstacles, we feel more confident about this book of the church. The seed of God's word at work within us has an effect when we cultivate it in our hearts and allow it to produce results within our lives. Paul spoke about this word in his letter to the Thessalonians, distinguishing it from a human word. With gratitude to his readers for their open hearts, he says:

> "We constantly give thanks to God for this, that when you received the word of God that you heard from us, you accepted it not as a human word but as what it really is, God's word, which is also at work in you believers." (1 Thess 2:13)

This word of God can work within us when we reflectively study and pray the sacred Scriptures. The effects of the word within us are usually subtle but real. The more we remove the obstacles in the way — our fears, impatience, temptations, difficulties, our lack of understanding — the more we will experience the transforming effects of the word of God.

Studying the Book of the Church

Because the Bible is the sacred literature of God's people, the book of the church, we must make every effort as communities of faith to encourage one another to read the Bible regularly and to teach each other how to reflect on these texts in a way that makes them a living word for our lives. A fully renewed and evangelized church can only come about when Catholics learn to encounter Christ through sacred Scripture and let the Holy Spirit move us to witness.

Many believe that the best form of Scripture study for Catholics focuses on the Lectionary readings for Sunday Mass. These are the sections read at the church's public worship, and over the cycles of three years they cover a good portion of the Bible. When these readings are studied and pondered during the week before the Sunday liturgy, the proclaimed Scriptures are heard with greater depth and understanding. When small faith communities reflect and pray with these readings during the week, their experience with the wider community on Sundays is enlivened and enriched. Even better, when the priests or deacons who will deliver the Sunday homilies can listen to members of the congregation discuss these Scriptures in the context of their lives, the ability of the homilist to touch the hearts of their congregation and apply the Scriptures to the daily discipleship of their parishioners will be enhanced.[42]

> **When communities of faith begin to study the Bible together, profound changes occur in the way people relate to one another.**

There are drawbacks, however, with basing parish Bible study exclusively on the Lectionary readings. Although the Lectionary presents a good bit of the Bible over the course of three years, large parts of the Bible are not contained in the church's Sunday readings. In addition, these readings are excerpts from the Bible, and as excerpts, they are lifted out of their biblical context. The liturgical readings presume that the hearers know the context. When we read a piece of Israel's history in the first reading, we understand the text if we are familiar with the book of the Torah or prophets from which it is taken. When the people of Israel sang the psalms, they knew the names, places, and events to which the psalms refer. And so should we. The letters of the New Testament presume that we know the basic theology of Paul, Peter, and John, so that we can understand the ideas referred to in the portion selected for the liturgy. When the gospel is proclaimed, we should recognize its place in the whole ministry of Jesus and have an understanding of the complete gospel that forms its context.

Good Catholic commentaries can be read by those who have the time and ability to study the individual books of the Bi-

---

42   See Stephen J. Binz, *Conversing with God in Advent and Christmas* (Frederick, MD: The Word Among Us Press, 2012); *Conversing with God in Lent* (Frederick, MD: The Word Among Us Press, 2010); *Conversing with God in the Easter Season* (Frederick, MD: The Word Among Us Press, 2013). Each volume is subtitled *Praying the Sunday Mass Readings with Lectio Divina.*

ble. The new *Catholic Commentary on Sacred Scripture* is a solid multi-volume commentary on the books of the New Testament.[43] It provides informative commentary and helps Catholics integrate Scripture with doctrine, worship, and daily life. The *New Collegeville Bible Commentary* provides small volumes on each book of the Bible, written in a pastoral style.[44] In addition, each volume contains an index of citations from the *Catechism of the Catholic Church* within that biblical book.

Other ways of engaging with the Bible include studies based on topics, themes, and persons of the Bible. Generally these types of studies include selected passages from a variety of biblical books. A study of a biblical theme can enrich one's understanding in a unique way by focusing on the many ways the theme is presented by various authors and writings.[45] A study of biblical personages explores the way God worked through particular characters to mold their lives as instruments of his kingdom.[46] By studying these biblical heroes across several biblical books and through different perspectives, they can become mentors and inspirations for our own journey of discipleship.

When communities of faith begin to study the Bible together, profound changes occur in the way people relate to one another. Individuals better understand their purpose as disciples of Jesus. Communities understand the meaning of their life together as a people united in the mission of the Lord. When parishioners meet one another on the street corner, they might not occupy their time by chatting about the weather, but might mention what they've

---

43   *Catholic Commentary on Sacred Scripture*, 17 volumes, edited by Peter S. Williamson and Mary Healy (Grand Rapids: Baker Academic).

44   *New Collegeville Bible Commentary*, edited by Daniel Durken, O.S.B. (Collegeville, MN: Liturgical Press). Many of these volumes may be used with a Study Guide developed by Little Rock Scripture Study for parish study.

45   A variety of thematic studies may be found at *Threshold Bible Study*, written by Stephen J. Binz (New London, CT: Twenty-Third Publications).

46   See *Ancient-Future Bible Study*, written by Stephen J. Binz (Grand Rapids: Brazos Press). Current books include studies of Abraham, David, Women of the Torah, Women of the Gospels, Peter, and Paul.

been reading about in Scripture. That would indeed be a sign of a community formed by the word and enlivened in the Spirit.

Other Ways of Forming Communities of the Word

The Bible must no longer be a closed, dusty book on the shelves of Catholic homes. As the book of the church, the Bible must be honored, read, discussed, and lived. Throughout the church's long history, the open book of the Scriptures has been the honored symbol of God's living word present in our midst. One way of encouraging this central place of Scripture in Catholic life is promoting the practice of Bible enthronement in Catholic homes.[47]

The open Bible, enthroned at church councils, in cathedrals and parish churches, and in Christian homes, bespeaks a rich tradition. At the Council of Ephesus in the fifth century, the Scriptures were enthroned in the midst of the bishops as they prayed for the guidance of the Holy Spirit. This tradition continued down through the centuries, and again at the Second Vatican Council, the open book of the Scriptures was enthroned as a sign of Christ's presence during the deliberations in St. Peter's Basilica. Processions, candles, bowing, and incense all express our church's reverence for the inspired word as it is enthroned, opened, and proclaimed in Catholic worship.

We can continue this ancient tradition of Bible enthronement in our own homes. Just as we set the sacred Scriptures in a place of honor in our churches, we can place the Holy Bible in an honorable location in our homes. Every Catholic home is a "domestic church." The Bible enthroned in our homes is a continual reminder that God's word speaks to us in the joys and struggles of everyday life. As the church constantly finds its nourishment and strength in sacred Scripture, so the word of God can bring comfort, challenge, inspiration, and guidance to every home.

The worldwide Catholic Biblical Federation has promoted for many years the practice of Bible Sunday, setting aside a special Sunday in the church's liturgical year to stress the importance of

---

47   A sample prayer service called "Enthrone the Bible in Your Home" may be downloaded at http://pastoralplanning.com/TBS/Enthrone_the_Bible_at_Home.pdf

the Bible. This special celebration might be in conjunction with a biblical art contest for children, a special speaker for the parish, or the launch of a parishwide Bible study. At the Sunday Mass, people are asked to bring their own Bibles, and the celebrant offers a special encouragement and blessing over the Bibles. People publically commit themselves to God's word, and then they are encouraged to return home to enthrone their Bibles and to begin the practice of personal and family reading.

The word of God is not just contained in the biblical page. Biblical music, drama, painting, sculpture, and other forms of art can creatively express God's word, a word that can never be contained or enclosed. Although we greatly venerate the sacred texts, the Christian faith is not a "religion of the book": Christianity rather is the "religion of the word of God," not of "a written and mute word, but of the incarnate and living Word."[48] Although we should always teach people how to read the text, there are countless ways of experiencing God's word and creating a biblical imagination in the people of God.

As we continue to remove the obstacles that prevent our Catholic parishes from becoming communities of the word, let us realize that studying Scripture is certainly nothing new for Catholics when considering the church's long tradition. St. Jerome, in the fourth century, said: "Ignorance of the Scriptures is ignorance of Christ." There is no better reason to encourage Catholic Christians to learn from Scripture. We listen to God's word in Scripture so that we might know Jesus Christ, live more deeply in him, and be witnesses of his reign in the world.

Reading the Bible Anew

Standing outside a Gothic church, a viewer can see the arches and the stained glass windows and get some idea of their lofty form. But it is only when the archways and windows are seen from inside the church that the full magnificence of their structure, pattern, light, and color can be experienced. The same is true with the Bible. Certainly readers can sense something of the richness of

---

48   Bernard of Clairvaux, *Homilia super missus est*, IV, 11; *Patrologia Latina* 183, 86.

the texts when read from outside the believing community of the church. But only when Scripture is heard within the context of the church's faith and worship can it be experienced in all its splendor as God's living word.

Easy answers put us in control and allow us to change others, instead of allowing God to change us and mold our lives.

Reading the Scriptures as an outsider, without the context of faith and the church, can lead to distorted understandings of what the Bible is. Some people think that it is a text that condemns us. Burdened by a sense of shame and guilt, convinced that God could never love them, they selectively choose texts that show God inflicting plagues, displaying his wrath, and ready to punish sinners. Others are convinced that the purpose of the Bible is to confine us. They are convinced they would be free and happy if only God were not imposing arbitrary laws and obstructing the lives of his subjected people. Then there are those who come to the Bible thinking that it is designed to correct us. They are convinced that God will embrace us just as soon as we straighten out our lives and become acceptable to him. So they think that the Bible is essentially a collection of commandments, principles, precepts, and ethical lessons. Still others believe that the Bible is meant to comfort us. They see it as an anthology of pleasant sayings, miraculous deeds, and wonderful stories, all designed to lift us up and give us a boost as we struggle through gloomy days.

But the Bible is not intended to condemn us or confine us. Nor is it intended primarily to correct us or even to comfort us. Rather, its purpose is to captivate us. Reading Scripture within the context of faith and the church enables us to experience God speaking to us and drawing us to himself. Listening to the sacred texts with the guidance of the same Holy Spirit who inspired them enables us to read Scripture from the inside rather than from the outside. Experiencing God's word within the community of faith enables us to experience God's word in all its splendor and captivating power.

We've got to learn to read the Bible in a way that doesn't require that we have all the answers. We need to realize that the need we feel to figure it all out and the frustration we feel when we can't completely understand a passage are simply a result of our modern, Western way of thinking. Jesus was asked a lot of questions during his public ministry. If you count up all the questions asked of Jesus in the gospels, you would find well over a hundred. But how many questions did Jesus answer? Well, not many. Jesus usually did one of three things when asked a question: he remained silent, as when Pilate questioned Jesus at his trial; or he responded with another question, as he did when he asked whose head is on the coin when questioned about paying taxes to Caesar; or he told a story, as he did in telling the parable of the Good Samaritan when asked "Who is my neighbor?"

Many people think that the purpose of religion and of studying the Bible is to find answers. But while easy answers might satisfy our curiosity occasionally, they don't allow God to change us. Jesus' understanding of God's word and of his church does not involve dispensing answers to people. Rather it is about leading them into the experience of God's life, where people seek wisdom and transformation, where hearts are changed and lives are rearranged. Easy answers put us in control and allow us to change others, instead of allowing God to change us and mold our lives.

Over the years, I've been on several study trips to Latin America, Africa, and Asia. The purpose of those trips was to experience how people read the Bible in community in the developing world. And I am forever fascinated by the insights and wisdom that come from simple, often uneducated people when reading Scripture, reflecting on it with others, and responding in prayer and action. These people in developing nations express thoughts and applications from Scripture passages that people in the developed Western world would never even think of. In situations of struggle, people tend to read the Bible much more with a view toward transformation rather than acquiring answers.

I have experienced so often in poor people the same response that the two disciples on the road to Emmaus felt when opening the Scriptures in the presence of Jesus: "Were not our hearts burning within us?" It is so much easier to encounter Jesus and experience

Scripture as the word of God when we don't have so many obstacles in the way. We've got to realize how much our riches, our Western culture, our rationalistic patterns of thought, and our consumerist lifestyles impede us from experiencing the life of God through the inspired word.

When we read Scripture, we ought to be interested not so much in knowing more but in becoming more. We need to focus on reading the Bible formatively, so that the Holy Spirit uses it to form Christ in us. Engaging with God's word within the Spirit-guided community of faith has profound consequences for life: transforming understandings, attitudes, and worldviews, impelling people in new directions, drawing people into a renewed relationship with God.

**In this age of the New Evangelization,
Catholic Bible study is more essential than ever.**

Although God's revelation is unchangeable and addressed to all people, the Holy Spirit speaks through it in every age. The Spirit illumines the minds of people in every culture to receive Scripture freshly. The ancient words of Scripture continually take on new life as they intersect with the unique circumstances and needs of each person and community. As long as we continue to take away the obstacles to the growth of God's word, the inspired texts will change hearts and lives and renew God's people in Christ.

Throughout most of the church's history the Bible was proclaimed and heard primarily in community. It was only with the invention of the printing press in the fifteenth century that Bibles could be put into the hands of individuals. In fact, the Gutenberg Bible in Latin was the first book ever printed. Of course, this ability to mass-produce Bibles was a wonderful thing, yet it did have its downside. Access to the Bible in print has led people to an increasingly individualistic interaction with Scripture. Individual response to the gospel has tended to become ever more important, eroding the essential communal nature of faith. When people read Scripture apart from the community, they tend to read for personal comfort or individual knowledge. Individualistic Bible reading can lessen the relational quality of God's word, our sense of being addressed by God who speaks and commands us to listen. We can forget that God addresses us for a purpose — that of shaping us to be his own people who are called to be light for the world and instruments of his kingdom.

In contrast to this individualizing tendency, Catholic teaching encourages us to place the Bible at the center of all the preaching and catechetical efforts of our church. The exhortations of the Second Vatican Council are now enshrined in the *Catechism of the Catholic Church*:

> All the preaching of the church, as indeed the entire Christian religion, should be nourished and ruled by sacred Scripture. Such is the force and power of the word of God that it can serve the church as her support and vigor and the children of the church as strength for their faith, food for the soul, and a pure and lasting font of spiritual life.... Hence, access to sacred Scripture ought to be open wide to the Christian faithful.[49]

This biblical renewal in the church is one of the great accomplishments of the council and of the church in our day. Yet, the church also has a long way to go in this regard. In this age of the New Evangelization, Catholic Bible study is more essential than ever. As more and more Catholics begin studying the Bible and putting it at the center of their life of prayer, the church will certainly find its way into the future. With catechesis and spirituality rooted in the Scriptures, we will understand God's will ever more clearly and continue becoming the church that Christ founded us to be.

For Reflection or Discussion

1. What has been your experience of Catholic Bible study in your parish or community? What would you like to see happen in the future?

2. How can you express reverence for the Scriptures, in liturgy, in your community, and in your home?

---

49   *Dei Verbum*, 21–22; CCC 131.

3. What are some of the obstacles today that block the seed of God's word from putting down roots, shooting upward, and bearing flowers and fruit?

4. What are the biggest obstacles you experience in your desire to study Scripture? What realizations help you the most?

5. What are some of the false or distorted understandings some people have about the Bible in our society?

6. In what ways does your culture affect the way you read the Bible? How can you read the Bible less for information and more for transformation?

7. What are the dangers of exclusively individual Bible reading? Why must the Bible always be read in the context of God's people?

Chapter 8

Lectio Divina for Evangelization

If we are to be an evangelizing church, witnessing to the reign of God in the world, we must not only imagine a better future but we must recover some of the wisdom of the past. The church of the first few centuries offers a richness of Christian experience that has been lost in many places. But, the church today is recovering many of these ancient practices, not only through the movement within Catholicism of *resourcement* (retrieving the ancient sources), but also through the emerging ecumenical friendship between the Catholic and Orthodox traditions, and through similar interests within Protestant and Evangelical Christianity. As the common tradition of all followers of Jesus, the early centuries offer us practices to rediscover, like liturgy, sacramental initiation, patristic insight, ascetic practices, contemplative prayer, and certainly, lectio divina.

By approaching the sacred text with faith, openheartedness, reverence, and expectation, we open ourselves to God's self-offering and respond with our hearts.

As a way of praying, lectio divina honors that most basic source of all real prayer — an interior desire for God. Lectio divina lets us understand that our desire for God is the result of God's initiative, the stirring of God's grace within us, drawing us and inviting us to a deeper intimacy with him. By beginning with the revealed word of God, lectio divina continues the conversation that God has begun. We first pay attention to his approach to us and focus on our receptivity. Scripture becomes a means for God to feed, heal, and love us. By approaching the sacred text with faith, openheartedness, reverence, and expectation, we open ourselves to God's self-offering and respond with our hearts.[50]

Although the term "lectio divina" (sacred reading) is not found in ecclesial writings until the third century, this way of reading Scripture is our inheritance from the Jewish tradition and is the church's most ancient way of reading Scripture. Jewish teachers taught their disciples to immerse themselves in prayerful reading of the sacred scrolls. Because the text itself is sacred, the ark containing the biblical scrolls is sacred space in the synagogue, with lamps burning around it, proclaiming God's holy presence. And the Jewish people know that they open themselves to that presence of God through reading, meditation, and prayer of the Torah, prophets, and writings of Scripture.

The term is found extensively in the patristic writings in the third through the fifth centuries, beginning with Origen. St. Jerome urged his hearers to feed the soul each day with lectio divina.[51] This practice nourished the fathers and mothers of the desert in these early centuries and then entered the emerging monastic movement. In the West, St. Benedict incorporated lectio divina into his Rule for the monastic life.

By the high Middle Ages, unfortunately, this personal reading of Scripture declined in the church, especially outside the monasteries. The Scholastic method of theology became increasingly suspicious of personal experience and the contemplative dimensions of prayer. During this period, a book by a Carthusian monk named Guigo II, entitled *The Monk's Ladder,* described lectio divina as four rungs on an ascending ladder on which monks are "lifted up from earth to heaven." Each rung represents an in-

---

50   See Stephen J. Binz, *Conversing with God in Scripture: A Contemporary Approach to Lectio Divina* (Frederick, MD: The Word Among Us Press, 2008).

51   Jerome, *Commentaries on Isaiah,* 18, Prologue: *Patrologia Latina* 24, 17b.

creasingly higher and more difficult "step"[52] The higher rungs are for those who have special graces, and contemplation was identified with extraordinary mystical states, something to be admired by lay people from a safe distance. This systematizing of the tradition represented a striking departure from the more ancient practice, and partly explains why lectio divina went out of favor for many centuries in the church.

Today, however, lectio divina is experiencing a worldwide revival as Christians everywhere are returning to this age-old wisdom to experience Scripture in a deeper and more complete way. There is no single method for the practice of lectio divina. It is not a rigid step-by-step system for encountering God in biblical passages. The spiritual masters of the early church never trusted methods of prayer and spiritual practice that were too rigidly defined. They always wanted to make room for the freedom necessary to respond to the Spirit's promptings.

In my own writing about lectio divina, I have incorporated what I call five "movements." Comparable to the movements in a classical work of music, each movement has its own characteristics and can even be practiced independently of the others. There is plenty of room for personal interpretation within the tradition. Listening, meditation, prayer, contemplation, and witness, individually and together, contribute to the full experience of lectio divina. Through the movements, we are led to an encounter with God who speaks to us through the pages of the inspired text, inviting from us a personal response and a gradual transformation of life.

Listening — Reading the Text with Expectation

Reading a sacred text in this tradition means reading with expectancy, trusting that God will speak his word to us through the page. St. Benedict, in his monastic Rule, described this kind of

---

52   *Scala Claustralium, Sources Chretiennes* 163 (Paris: Cerf, 1942); *The Ladder of the Monks and Twelve Meditations by Guigo II* (Garden City, NY: Doubleday Image, 1978).

reading as hearing "with the ear of our heart."[53] God speaks, and we listen.

The key to this deep listening is reading the biblical text with as little prejudgment as possible, as if we were hearing it for the first time. We can't listen fully to God if we think we already know what the text is going to tell us. Rather, this expectant reading requires that we create a space within ourselves for the new insight and wisdom God wants to give us through the sacred page.

This deep listening requires careful, fully attentive reading, engaging our mind, our imagination, our emotions, and our will. It can be helpful to read aloud, so that we see the words with our eyes, form them with our lips, and hear them with our ears. We savor the words of the sacred literature, appreciating the images, envisioning the scene, feeling the sentiments, allowing the words to move from our heads to our hearts. St. Ambrose urged readers to avoid the tendency to read large passages in haste: "We should read not in agitation, but in calm; not hurriedly, but slowly, a few words at a time, pausing in attentive reflection.... Then the readers will experience their ability to enkindle the ardor of prayer."[54]

Seeking to comprehend the meaning of a text is an important part of encountering God there and being changed by that encounter. The Jewish rabbis and the church's patristic theologians show us that there is no clear distinction between studying Scripture and reading it prayerfully. The more we come to understand the text with our minds, the more we are capable of being changed by the text.

We will be able to probe the fullest meaning of the text the more we comprehend something of its original context — historical, cultural, literary, and religious. When, where, and why was the author writing? Most importantly, how did the writer's faith manifest itself in the text and what kind of faith response does the writer expect from the reader? Seeking to understand the faith dimension of the text helps us transcend the original circumstances in which it was written and allows us to see the lasting significance and validity it has for all of us.

---

53   Benedict, *The Rule of Saint Benedict*, Prologue.

54   Ambrose, *Orationes sive meditationes*, Prologue.

Bible studies and biblical commentaries can be a great help to understanding. Listening to the text with the understanding of the church and with some basic insights of biblical scholarship can assure us that our comprehension is true and faithful. This listening to the text for understanding, with its multiple layers of meaning and rich history of interpretation, forms the foundation on which we can begin to experience its transforming potential.

With expectant listening, the words of Scripture become the means of God speaking to us. As God's Spirit guided the human authors to express the truth that God wished to entrust to the Scriptures, God also guides us through that same Spirit as we read the Bible as God's word to us.

Meditation — Reflecting on the Meaning and Message of the Text

Even though the Bible, was written ages ago, its pages always have meanings and messages for us today. Our challenge is to find connections between the text of yesterday and the today of our lives. By reflecting on the sacred texts, we link the biblical truth of scriptural passages to the experience of faith in the world in which we live.

Reading the Bible we often encounter a wall that divides the text of the past from our lives today. That wall is created by the difference in time, language, culture, and experience between the world in which the Bible was written and our own contemporary world. By meditating on the text, we begin to break down that wall between the sacred text, written so long ago, and our own lives today.

Because the biblical literature is the word of God, it has a richness of meaning that can be discovered by individuals in every age and in every culture.

When the patristic writers of the early church interpreted the Bible, they considered their work incomplete until they had found a meaning in the text that was relevant to the situation of Christians in their own day. Because the biblical literature is the word of God, it has a richness of meaning that can be discovered by individuals in every age and in every culture. Its personal message can be received by every reader who listens to the word in the context of his or her daily experiences. We should read the text until it becomes like a mirror, reflecting some of our own thoughts, questions, challenges, and experiences. We know that our meditation is fruitful when we come to realize that God is trying to speak personally to us and offer us a message through the scriptural text.

After hearing a work of music that has moved us, we naturally want to reflect on it, letting it echo within us. After reading a poem that strikes us deeply, we want to pause in silence to allow it to resonate and complete its work in us. This should be our response to the sacred text when we allow Christ to speak to us and guide us through his Spirit. We want to create a space in our hearts for God's word to reside. To practice meditation well is to let the Scriptures take root in us, penetrating the deepest part of our being so that they become part of us.

The more we meditate on God's word, the more it seeps into our lives and saturates our thoughts and feelings. St. Ambrose described how this assimilation takes place: "When we drink from sacred Scripture, the life-sap of the eternal Word penetrates the veins of our soul and our inner faculties."[55] Meditation allows the dynamic word of God to so penetrate our lives that it truly infuses our minds and hearts and we begin to embody its truth, goodness, and beauty.

Praying — Responding to God's Word from the Heart

After listening carefully and reflectively to God's word in Scripture, we naturally reach a point in which we want to respond to the One whose voice we have heard. This is the movement of prayer, our heartfelt response to God's word. Lectio divina, then, becomes fundamentally a dialogue with God: we listen to God, and then we respond to God in prayer.

This type of prayer flows directly from our experience of listening to and meditating on the word of God. It is not just repeated

---

55   Ambrose, *Commentaries on the Psalms I*, 33: *Patrologia Latina* 14, 984.

formulas. Rather, the biblical vocabulary, images, and sentiments of the biblical text are joined with the thoughts, needs, and desires arising within us. Our personal prayer is enriched through the inspired words of the biblical tradition.

When we first open ourselves to hear God's voice through his word, we are able to respond with a more grace-filled and Spirit-led prayer to God.

Depending on what we have heard God saying to us in our listening and meditation, our prayer may be an act of praise or thanksgiving, of petition or repentance. In some cases, our prayer may even be a rebellion, a crying lament, or an angry tirade, as we see in the literature of Job, Jeremiah, and some of the psalms. In any case, the key is that our prayerful response to God flows directly from our listening. This prevents our prayer from becoming routine or repetitive. It is always a fresh prayer spontaneously arising from the heart.

This prayer from the heart shows us the proper order of listening and praying. Sometimes we tend to pray first, telling God how we feel and what we need, and then we wait for God to answer. This prayer teaches us that listening comes first. When we first open ourselves to hear God's voice through his word, we are able to respond with a more grace-filled and Spirit-led prayer to God. In this way our prayer becomes increasingly personal and intimate, resonating with the faith, hope, and love that animated the characters and writers of the Bible in their journey with God.

This prayer is not only our own response to God, but it is also a gift of God. Left to ourselves, without God's grace, we would not be able to pray at all. The sin of our humanity has weakened our natural desire to pray, and we tend to hide from God and avoid intimacy with him. But God did not create us this way, and he wants to have a deep personal relationship with each one of us.

Because of God's love for us, he takes the initiative in forming a bond with us. He uses Scripture to help us see ourselves as he sees us and to tell us of his loving care for us. He invites us into a dialogue with himself, a listening and responding, as between intimate friends.

In the Sermon on the Mount, Jesus urged his disciples to pray in the private recesses of their home: "Whenever you pray, go into your room and shut the door and pray to your Father who is in secret" (Mt 6:6). Ancient commentators understood this "inner room" as an image of the human heart, our center and our most personal dwelling. This secret place that God alone can see is the most fruitful place for prayer.

When we discover an ability and desire to pray within our hearts, we know that it is a gift of the Holy Spirit. Paul's letter to the Romans speaks to the uncertainty we have about our ability to pray and our fearfulness about praying well:

> Likewise the Spirit helps us in our weakness; for we do not know how to pray as we ought, but that very Spirit intercedes with sighs too deep for words. And God, who searches the heart, knows what is the mind of the Spirit, because the Spirit intercedes for the saints according to the will of God. (Rom 8:26–27)

We all know our weaknesses when it comes to prayer. Our false self-sufficiency and need for control can stifle the life and grace and the gifts of the Holy Spirit within us. But if we let him take control, God promises us that his divine Spirit will come into our hearts and pray within us. Since God alone can see our hearts, he receives our Spirit-guided prayer and gives us all that we need according to his loving plan for us.

This prayer is our active effort to keep our hearts open to God's Spirit by preparing the way for his work within us. Our desire is all-important. In fact, St. Augustine said, "The desire to pray is itself prayer."[56] We discover the gift of prayer when we recover our desire for God. And we eventually realize that our desire for God is itself the presence of his Spirit working within us.

Contemplation — Quietly Resting in God

The previous movements of lectio divina have all involved the use of words. In listening we carefully read the words of Scripture. In

---

56   Augustine, *Explanations of the Psalms*, 37, 14: *Patrologia Latina* 36, 404.

meditation we reflect on the implications of those inspired words for our own lives. In prayer we respond to God's word with words of our own. But eventually, in this prayerful process, words become unnecessary and no longer helpful; they have taken us as far as they can. The movement of contemplation is mostly wordless silence, an effortless resting in God. We simply end our prayer by receiving and accepting the transforming embrace of the One who has led us to this moment.

Contemplation requires that we let go of any effort to be in charge of the process. When we feel God drawing us into a deeper awareness of his divine presence, we gradually abandon our intellectual activity and let ourselves be wooed into God's embrace. We no longer have to think or reason, listen or speak. Moments of this kind of wordless presence occur in any loving relationship. The experience resembles that of lovers holding each other in wordless silence or of a sleeping child resting in her mother's arms.

The movement of contemplation is mostly wordless silence, an effortless resting in God.

Contemplation is more difficult to experience today than in previous ages. Because of the mind-set of our culture, we define people primarily by their "doing" rather and their "being." We judge our own life and that of others by successes and achievements. According to this way of thinking, simply being in the presence of God without accomplishing anything seems like a waste of time to many people. All the material and technological accomplishments of the twenty-first century are not without their price. Never before in history have people been so prone to analyze, intellectualize, and control everything about life. The analytical faculties of our minds overshadow the intuitive faculties that we need so much for contemplation. Our pragmatic intellects have triumphed over the receptive intuition that brings us into communion with the divine.

Saints and theologians of earlier centuries considered contemplation as part of the normal experience of prayer for most Christians. Most considered it a higher stage, reached along the road of receptive listening and vocal prayer, but they believed it was a natural phase of prayer available to anyone with an open heart. But because of our contemporary mind-set, the development of contemplation seems far less natural and spontaneous than it was in previous centuries, and people today often exclude contemplation from their prayer.

In contrast to the rapid, noisy communication of our technological world, quiet, receptive stillness is the atmosphere in which the most important communication occurs.

This lack of appreciation for "being" and our overvalued emphasis on "doing" has created a void that explains the attraction for Eastern spirituality today. People are searching for a greater spiritual depth than our culture offers. We long for a way to relate to God that does not depend on what we do and what we accomplish, but on who we are at the deepest level. This is the kind of mindfulness and awareness of the divine that contemplation can give us. Although the practice of contemplation seems passive and "useless" from a practical point of view, we can trust that God is acting within us. When we humbly expose our heart, the center of our being, to God, what happens within us during those moments is not up to us. God's grace is truly at work in those moments, and the Holy Spirit is changing us without our direct knowledge or understanding.

In contrast to the rapid, noisy communication of our technological world, quiet, receptive stillness is the atmosphere in which the most important communication occurs. If we spend all of our time in extroverted activity, we become strangers to our own inner life. By denying ourselves the environment in which to cultivate contemplation, we deny ourselves a fuller understanding of our true self and the personal transformation made possible through a deeper relationship with God.

Witness — Faithful Living in Christ

In addition to drawing us inward to reflection and prayer, the word of God impels us outward to those people and situations in need of God's light and compassionate presence. Witness is our lived response to the biblical text. The practice of lectio divina leads to evangelization.

Our listening to Scripture must have an effect beyond the prayerful exercise itself. Through lectio divina we evangelize ourselves; or better, we allow God to evangelize us through his inspired word. Every biblical text offers a challenge to those who hear it. It calls us to become witnesses of God's kingdom and members of the body of Christ in the world.

Our human reason and experience must always accompany our prayerful discernment as we decide how to live out the word of God.

We cannot listen to God's word and reflectively pray with Scripture without being changed in some specific way. As we deepen our relationship with God through the movements of lectio divina, our actions become vehicles of his presence to others. We become channels of God's mercy, becoming "doers of the word and not merely hearers" (Jas 1:22), bringing about God's loving purposes in our daily lives. Living out the word that we have heard in our hearts can be as simple as helping a person in need or being kind to someone we don't like. It can be as demanding as a call to reconcile with someone who is estranged from us or an urge to change some aspect of our career.

God's word not only communicates ideas, it also contains the power to create change. Just as the integrity of any person's word is weighed not only by the ideas it contains but by the results it achieves, so the word that goes forth from God achieves its purpose. In a beautiful poetic metaphor, Isaiah speaks about God's word as a penetrating rain and blanketing snow, giving moisture to the earth so that it may bear fruit:

> For as the rain and the snow come down from heaven,
>   and do not return there until they have watered
>   the earth,
> making it bring forth and sprout,
>   giving seed to the sower and bread to the eater,

so shall my word be that goes out from my mouth;
it shall not return to me empty,
but it shall accomplish that which I purpose,
and succeed in the thing for which I sent it. (Isa 55:10–11)

As the rain and the snow fall to the earth, they meet a yearning receptivity. The ground receives their welcome moisture as an assurance that the seed will sprout and eventually bear fruit. Sometimes God's word falls on deaf ears or distracted minds. But if we listen and open our hearts, eventually that word will penetrate the parched soil of our lives. Not only will God's word refresh us and help us to grow, it will cause us to bear the fruit that God intends for us to share.

All the other movements of lectio divina are necessary to experience before the witness of our lived response. We cannot simply move from reading Scripture to acting in the world. The Bible is not a collection of maxims to be put into practice. Rarely does Scripture offer us concrete details about what to do in specific situations. Our human reason and experience must always accompany our prayerful discernment as we decide how to live out the word of God. Paul desired this discernment for all Christ's disciples: "Be transformed by the renewal of your minds, so that you may discern what is the will of God — what is good and acceptable and perfect" (Rom 12:2). Listening, meditation, prayer, and contemplation are all necessary components of this discernment. Lectio divina shapes our being and thereby shapes our action. From this process of personal renewal flows the witness of Christian discipleship and evangelization.

Evangelizers as Contemplative Witnesses

We can expand Jesus' image of the seed as the word of God to the movements of lectio divina. Listening is the sprouting of the plant, and meditation is the leafing. In a healthy plant, prayer and contemplation are surely the budding and the blossoming. Extending this metaphor through the cycle of life, witness is the delicate fruit that gradually ripens on the healthy plant rooted in God's word. The fertile blossom and the ripened fruit, of course, bring forth new seeds for the growth of new plants as the cycle of lectio divina continues.

Of course any gardener will tell you that the blossom and the fruit are the most wonderful results of this process of growth. But if asked to choose the most beautiful — the blossom or the fruit — the one who loves the plant would be hard pressed to decide. Of course, they are both beautiful, wonderful, and necessary. Likewise, in the practice of lectio divina, both contemplative prayer and active witness grow together in a person who is engaging with the word of God.

If we are blind to God's presence in the world of our family and our work, in political action and work for justice, contemplation opens our eyes.

Those who would favor the blossom might argue that there is no greater experience than unity with God. This should be the goal of all reflection and prayer. But those who favor the fruit might propose that our engagement with God's word cannot be complete until we make a difference in the world or in the life of another person. Of course, both of these perspectives are correct. The word of God draws us inward, and it impels us outward.

The life of Jesus shows us this two-way movement most compellingly as he both goes away in solitude to commune with the Father and brings the good news of God's reign to the people. The lives of the saints convince us that contemplation and witness cannot be separated in the lives of Jesus' followers. Both are necessary and develop together in the hearts of genuine disciples. We do not have one heart for God and another for human beings. Throughout history many of the most ardent activists have been the most fervent contemplatives.

Both contemplation and witness are necessary ingredients for Catholic evangelization. Contemplation does not separate us from the world and other people, and witness to Christ is not genuine unless it grows out of contemplation. Compassion and care for others arises from contemplation, and the call to evangelize arises out of a compassionate heart dedicated to the good of our neighbors. Contemplation enables us to realize that God is not absent from life's daily reality. If we are blind to God's presence in the world of our family and our work, in political action and work for justice, contemplation opens our eyes. Contemplation enables us to see the deepest meaning in issues, problems, and events. Through contemplation we savor the creative presence of God's word, and thereby open ourselves to become more deeply involved in the transformational process that God's word has provoked throughout history.

The gospels show us that Jesus first called people to discipleship, to learn from him and follow in his way. Only then did Jesus send them out to proclaim the kingdom in his name. Jesus' first command was "come" and his last command was "go." The same is true in the church today. The risen Christ calls men and women to come to him, to engage with God's word, and to learn to rest in God. And then he sends these disciples out to evangelize, to witness his good news to others.

The mystical poetry often attributed to St. Teresa of Ávila expresses what a contemplative witness knows:

> Christ has no body now but yours. No hands, no feet on earth but yours. Yours are the eyes through which he looks compassion on this world. Yours are the feet with which he walks to do good. Yours are the hands through which he blesses all the world. Yours are the hands, yours are the feet, yours are the eyes; you are his body. Christ has no body now on earth but yours.

Evangelizers live in Christ, and because they live in him, they witness and express his presence in the world. They can announce his good news only because they have become his new creation. Through the presence of the Holy Spirit, evangelizers are the feet through which the risen Christ does good and the hands through which he blesses all with grace and peace. Looking on the world with the compassionate eyes of Christ, evangelizers are his body now on earth.

For Reflection or Discussion

1. What does it mean to say that all real prayer is rooted in a personal desire for God? Why is this desire the foundation of lectio divina?

2. Why is the image of a ladder with steps reaching into heaven an unfortunate image for lectio divina?

3. Why is prejudgment of the biblical text an obstacle to genuine listening? How can you learn to listen with the ear of your heart?

4. In what sense is lectio divina essentially a dialogue with God? In this prayerful dialogue with God, why is it important to first listen before we respond in prayer?

5. Why does the dialogue of lectio divina eventually lead to wordless silence? Why might contemplation be particularly difficult today?

6. What is the connection between lectio divina and evangelization? Why must interior renewal come before external witness?

7. Why does effective evangelization require both contemplative prayer and active witness?

Chapter 9

Woman of the Word and Star of the New Evangelization

Throughout this book, we have considered how a renewed listening to Scripture must be the foundation of the New Evangelization. Now we reflect on two titles of Mary that point to her role in this mission of the church. The older title, Woman of the Word, points to Mary as a woman steeped in the Scriptures of Israel who conceived and gave birth to the Word of God. Her new title, Star of the New Evangelization, spotlights Mary as one who brings the Word of God to the world and announces the reign of her divine Son.

As Mary has always been the archetype for the church, she is the exemplar for us as we take up the mission of the church today. She shows us how to listen to the word of God, and so she is for us our model for lectio divina; she shows us how to witness to the word of God, and so she is our model for the New Evangelization. If we want Mary to be our guiding star for the New Evangelization, then we must first let her be our example of hearing God's word. Unless evangelization is rooted in the word and joined to biblical contemplation, it will become pure activism and soon run its course. Mary shows us how being contemplative witnesses to the gospel is the truest mission of every follower of her Son.

Hearing the Word of God and Doing It

Jesus' parable of the sower highlights the conditions in which people hear the word of God. Our receptivity to God's word depends on our clearing our lives of the obstacles that prevent the word from germinating and growing abundantly. Luke's gospel describes those who provide good soil as "the ones who, when they hear the word, hold it fast in an honest and good heart, and bear fruit with patient endurance" (Lk 8:15).

Immediately after the telling of this parable, Luke describes the approach of the mother and brothers of Jesus who are unable to reach Jesus because of the crowd. To this Jesus replies, "My mother and my brothers are those who hear the word of God and do it" (Lk 8:21). Jesus is saying that his family is those who create open hearts for the word of God to penetrate, take root, mature, and bear fruit.

As Mary has always been the archetype for the church, she is the exemplar for us as we take up the mission of the church today.

Jesus is not denying the biological role of Mary as his mother or his relationship with his close cousins or stepbrothers. But he insists that what is most important is hearing the word of God and doing it. Following in his way is not a matter of race or ethnicity, or even something we deserve or earn. All people can enter God's family by responding in faith to the word of God. Of course, Luke has already shown us in his opening chapters that Mary hears the word and acts on the word in an exemplary way.

Not only does Mary receive God's word and grow the infant Jesus in her own womb, but even more importantly, she receives the word of God into her very being. What we are called to imitate in Mary is this: she hears the word of God, she receives it deeply into her heart, she allows it to grow within her, and she bears Christ in witness to the world.

Luke shows us a similar scene a few chapters later in his gospel. A woman from the crowd raises her voice and says to Jesus, "Blessed is the womb that bore you and the breasts that nursed you!" But Jesus replies, "Blessed rather are those who hear the word of God and obey it!" (Lk 11:27–28). Yes, Mary bore Jesus in her womb and nursed him at her breasts. But we imitate Mary in that we prepare the soil of our lives, we receive the word of God into our deepest being, and we follow that word in obedience wherever it may lead us. This is discipleship. And Mary, as woman of the word, is the first and exemplary disciple.

The ancient tradition of lectio divina expresses our listening to the word of God, and the New Evangelization expresses our doing the word of God.

This combination of listening to the word of God and doing it is what our church is calling us to anew. The ancient tradition of lectio divina expresses our listening to the word of God, and the New Evangelization expresses our doing the word of God. This is what it means to be a disciple and an evangelizer. And in these two complementary roles, Mary is our model.

Lectio divina is listening to Scripture as the word of God and allowing it to do its work within us. Likewise, the New Evangelization is a way of living our baptismal call to be witnesses of Christ in the world. It means allowing ourselves to be evangelized by the word of God so that we can bring the good news of Jesus to others. This is the call that Luke offers us in the gospel: to be people of the word, to imitate Mary as the one who bore the word intimately in her heart and brought him forth for the world. She inspires us to listen, reflect, and do the word of God today.

Mary in the Mysteries of the Gospel

Many icons and ancient images of the Annunciation show Mary holding or reading Scripture when the angel is revealed to her. The image portrays Mary as woman of the word. Of course, the word for Mary of Nazareth was the Scriptures of Israel, what we Christians know as the Old Testament.

Mary listened to the Scriptures in many ways throughout her life. She was taught the stories of her ancestors by her parents. She heard the word proclaimed and chanted in the synagogue at Nazareth. When she and her family would travel to Jerusalem for the Jewish feasts, she would hear the Scriptures proclaimed and chanted in the temple. And she reflected and prayed with Scripture throughout her life. Mary's life was permeated by the Torah, the prophets, and the psalms.

Her attentive listening to the ancient Scriptures prepared her to receive the new divine revelation brought by the angel Gabriel.

> In the sixth month the angel Gabriel was sent by God to a town in Galilee called Nazareth, to a virgin engaged to a man whose name was Joseph, of the house of David. The virgin's name was Mary. And he came to her and said, "Greetings, favored one! The Lord is with you." But she was much perplexed by his words and pondered what sort of greeting this might be. The angel said to her, "Do not be afraid, Mary, for you have found favor with God. And now, you will conceive in your womb and bear a son, and you will name him Jesus. He will be great, and will be called the Son of the Most High, and the Lord God will give to him the throne of his ancestor David. He will reign over the house of Jacob forever, and of his kingdom there will be no end." Mary said to the angel, "How can this be, since I am a virgin?" The angel said to her, "The Holy Spirit will come upon you, and the power of the Most High will overshadow you; therefore the child to be born will be holy; he will be called Son of God." (Lk 1:26–35)

Because Mary was a woman of the word, she understood this language of revelation. She knew who the angel Gabriel was from his appearances in the prophecies of Daniel. She understood that the "house of David" was the descendants of King David from which the Messiah would be born. She remembered that others before her had been addressed by the words "The Lord is with you" when they were given a special role in God's plan. She had often addressed God as "the Most High" when she sang the Psalms. The one who will sit on "the throne of David" she knew from God's covenant with David is a title for the coming Messiah. She recognized that "the Holy Spirit" had come upon the prophets and others chosen to deliver God's word to his people. And she knew that "the Most High" had "overshadowed" the newly completed temple bringing to that earthly dwelling the glorious presence of God.

Yes, Mary, the woman of the word, knew that she was being called to participate in some wonderful way in the unfolding of salvation history. God had chosen her to be an instrument of his saving will for his people. And, of course, because she was a faithful daughter of Israel, she responded: "Here am I, the servant of the Lord; let it be with me according to your word" (Lk 1:38). Mary's attentive listening to the word of God had made her totally receptive to God's will. So she was able to respond to God with all her heart: "Here I am; let it be."

Mary, the woman of the word, knew that she was being called to participate in some wonderful way in the unfolding of salvation history.

Mary's response expresses her total compliance with God's plan, to be carried out through and in her. This openness to the Lord's word makes Mary the first and ideal disciple. The moment she articulated her availability to God's will and her acceptance of God's plan, God became flesh and dwelt among us. As in the tradition of lectio divina, Mary listened to God's word, she pondered that word, and she prayerfully responded to God.

Then immediately after her acceptance, Mary set out in haste to the Judean hill country, to witness to the word in the form of evangelization. In Mary's Visitation to Elizabeth, she shares the good news of the Incarnation.

> In those days Mary set out and went with haste to a Judean town in the hill country, where she entered the house of Zechariah and greeted Elizabeth. When Elizabeth heard Mary's greeting, the child leapt in her womb. And Elizabeth was filled with the Holy Spirit and exclaimed with a loud cry, "Blessed are you among women, and blessed is the fruit of your womb. And why has this happened to me, that the mother of my Lord comes to me? For as soon as I heard the sound of your greeting, the child in my womb leapt for joy. And blessed is she who believed that there would be a fulfillment of what was spoken to her by the Lord." (Lk 1:39–45)

Having received the word, Mary desires to share the word. She didn't just remain at home, preoccupied with her own life. She hurried to share the gospel with Elizabeth. She became the first evangelizer.

Luke's gospel is showing us that a true disciple will, like Mary, aspire to be an authentic evangelizer.

When Mary greeted Elizabeth, the child in Elizabeth's womb leapt for joy. Mary's very presence was an evangelizing graced moment both for Elizabeth and John the Baptist, still in the womb. This meeting of Elizabeth and Mary represents the ancient covenant and the new covenant coming together. The elderly Elizabeth, along with the elderly Zechariah, a priest of the temple in Jerusalem, represent God's work among the people of ancient Israel. The young, virginal Mary represents the new work that God is doing in sending the Messiah. The new honors the old, and the old esteems the new, showing the unity of God's saving plan.

Elizabeth proclaims that Mary is blessed by God in two ways. First, as the mother of Jesus: "Blessed are you among women, and blessed is the fruit of your womb." And second, as the model disciple: "Blessed is she who believed that there would be a fulfillment of what was spoken to her by the Lord." As both mother and disciple, we honor and imitate Mary, we learn from her and serve with her, and we worship her Son and rejoice in his presence.

Mary entered into the house of Zechariah and Elizabeth as the ideal evangelizer. She entered into their joys and sorrows, their blessings and burdens. And she stayed for three months. She didn't just announce the good news and then leave. Mary brought comfort and assurance to Elizabeth, and she confirmed her faith and helped her to trust.

Luke's gospel is showing us that a true disciple will, like Mary, aspire to be an authentic evangelizer. And, conversely, we cannot be successful evangelizers without being first a dedicated disciple. As the true disciple, Mary listens to the word, ponders it, and prays with it. As an authentic evangelizer, she responds to the word and witnesses to the word. She is the authentic model both for lectio divina and for the new evangelization.

During her visit with Elizabeth, Mary sang one of the most magnificent biblical prayers in Scripture, the Magnificat. This canticle of Mary demonstrates again that Mary has first interiorized God's word so that she can then proclaim God's word and testify to its work in her own life. Her soul magnifies the Lord as her spirit rejoices in praise and thanksgiving to God.

And Mary said,
"My soul magnifies the Lord,
    and my spirit rejoices in God my Savior,
for he has looked with favor on the lowliness of his servant.
        Surely, from now on all generations will call me blessed;
for the Mighty One has done great things for me,
    and holy is his name.
His mercy is for those who fear him
    from generation to generation.
He has shown strength with his arm;
        he has scattered the proud in the thoughts of
            their hearts.
He has brought down the powerful from their thrones,
    and lifted up the lowly;
he has filled the hungry with good things,
    and sent the rich away empty.
He has helped his servant Israel,
    in remembrance of his mercy,
according to the promise he made to our ancestors,
    to Abraham and to his descendants forever."
        (Lk 1:46–55)

One remarkable characteristic of the Magnificat is the way that Mary wove verses from the psalms and other Old Testament prayers into her own prayer. She had obviously learned these traditional prayers as a young girl as they were recited and chanted.

But Mary did not simply repeat the prayers of her ancestors; she prayed a completely new prayer that embodied both those ancient texts and the new divine word she had heard. By allowing God's word, both ancient and new, to interact with her own thoughts, feelings, memories, hopes, and desires, she gave voice to a beautiful biblical prayer that came from the depths of her heart. In this way, Mary is our model for prayer. As in the ancient tradition of lectio divina, Mary teaches us to first listen to God's word. Then, after pondering that word in our heart, we are able to respond to God in prayer.

So the Magnificat shows us Mary as Woman of the Word, but it also confirms that Mary is an evangelizer. She opened her mouth and gave praise and thanksgiving to God. She offered personal testimony of the great things that the Lord had done for her, and she proclaimed the gospel with the song that filled her heart. And her testimony and proclamation are meant to inspire her hearers with the hope that, as God has done great and wonderful things to an unknown village girl of Nazareth, God would do great and beautiful things in their lives as well.

Then, because Mary welcomed the word in her heart, and nourished the word in her very being, she was able to give birth to the word in the world. In the birth of Christ, as John's gospel tells us, "The Word became flesh and lived among us" (Jn 1:14). As the good soil accepts the seed, nurturing it until it sprouts forth and begins to flourish, Mary listens to the word, receives the word, ponders the word, allowing it to gestate in her very being. Then, she is able to go and witness to the word, and to give birth to the word in the world.

Like Mary and with Mary, we are called as disciples and evangelizers to make Christ incarnate in the world. By embodying the good news of salvation, by our witness, we make the Lord present to others. By the ways that we express joy and gratitude for what God has done for us, we become invitations to others to share in that same new life.

Mary as Exemplar of Lectio Divina

As Woman of the Word, Mary shows us how to listen to Scripture as the word of God, in a manner that is personal, prayerful, and transforming. This way of engaging with the inspired text, which the patristic theologians called lectio divina, allows the sacred texts to move from our heads to the depths of our hearts and to form us as a renewed people living in God's reign. Mary's life exemplifies each of the movements of lectio divina: listening, reflecting, praying, expectant waiting, and witnessing to her Son.

First, Mary shows us how to listen with expectation. In her home, in the synagogue, and in the temple, Mary listened to God's word and she sought to live according to its guidance. Because she was open to the new meaning that the ancient texts always offer, her attentive listening to the Scriptures of Israel prepared her to hear and receive the new divine revelation brought by the angel Gabriel. Gradually, she would come to understand that the sacred texts she had heard throughout her life were being fulfilled in her own life and in that of her Son. So, Mary teaches us how to listen to God's word with receptive and expectant devotion.

Mary's life exemplifies each of the movements of lectio divina: listening, reflecting, praying, expectant waiting, and witnessing to her Son.

Second, Mary shows us how to practice meditation, reflecting on the meaning and message of the text. Luke's gospel says, "Mary treasured all these words and pondered them in her heart" (Lk 2:19). Treasuring and pondering the word of God are the essence of meditation. Mary was a faithful disciple because she heard the word, treasured it, and pondered it in her heart. To "ponder" suggests that the word has enough gravity to shape and expand the understanding of the heart. So, she shows us how the word of God can form our hearts when we allow it to rest within us and gradually mold our desires, insights, and judgments.

Third, Mary shows us how to practice prayer from the heart. Because Mary had listened to God's word and learned to meditate on it, she was able to respond in prayer with her whole heart, "Let it be with me according to your word," and with her beautiful Magnificat. She integrated the words of the Scriptures of Israel with her own thoughts, feelings, and desires arising from her heart. Mary teaches us how to enrich our personal prayer with the inspired prayers of God's people throughout the ages.

Fourth, Mary shows us how to practice contemplation, quietly resting in God. By cultivating her prayer through an active relationship with Jesus throughout his life, Mary prepared for the silent and receptive waiting of contemplative prayer. After Jesus' resurrection and ascension, Mary waited with the other disciples for God to send the Holy Spirit: "All of these were constantly devoting themselves to prayer, together with Mary the mother of Jesus" (Acts 1:14). This confident and trustful waiting for the transforming work of the Holy Spirit is the model for the contemplative life.

As a model for our faithful witness, Mary offers us words of trust for our task of witnessing to the word.

Finally, Mary shows us how to witness faithfully in daily life. Mary's entire life was a response to the word of God, beginning with her youthful reply to the angel at the annunciation to the end of her life on earth. From Nazareth to Jerusalem, she was a faithful witness to the word, to which she had given her "yes; let it be." Even in her most difficult moments, standing beneath the cross of her son, Mary never retracted her commitment to live in total openness to God.

As a model for our faithful witness, Mary offers us words of trust for our task of witnessing to the word. At the beginning of Jesus' public ministry in John's gospel, Mary was with Jesus at a wedding feast in Cana. When the wine ran out, Mary instructed the servants, "Do whatever he tells you" (Jn 2:5). She knew that Jesus would transform their ordinary water into the vibrant wine of God's kingdom. As mother of the disciples after the resurrection, Mary tells us to prepare to do whatever Jesus asks of us. She knows that being "doers of the word" and responding to that word with trusting obedience is the way to our well-being and happiness. Through our witness, Jesus will take our ordinary lives and shape them into instruments for building his kingdom, making us his disciples and faithful evangelizers in the world today.

Star of the New Evangelization

A star is a celestial body that shines at night; Mary is our heavenly mother who shines in the darkness of ignorance, hopelessness, and void of meaning. She is a star of faith, a star of hope, a star of love. She shines as the Morning Star as night gives way to dawn. She shines on the horizon of salvation, preparing for the rising light of Jesus Christ.

We cannot profess faith in the Word made flesh without also proclaiming that he was conceived by the power of the Holy Spirit and born of the Virgin Mary. We cannot contemplate the saving cross of Jesus without remembering Mary, who participated in his suffering and whom Christ entrusted to his disciples before his death. We cannot declare our unity with the church without bearing in mind that Mary was present with the apostles at the first Pentecost when they were empowered to evangelize the world.

As we live in this age of the New Evangelization, we must consider how we can make the gospel of Jesus Christ compellingly attractive to men and women of our time.

Mary has an irreplaceable role in the history of salvation because she was present in all three of its phases: before Christ, during the life of Christ, and in the time of the church. Her maternal yes brought Christ into the world. She was uniquely associated with his redeeming mission, and she is mother of the church. Mary plays a vital active role in the passing from one phase of saving history to another. And, united with her Son, she has remained with the church in every generation.

The desire of every evangelizer is to bring others to Jesus Christ. Mary is the star that leads and guides wise men and women to find and encounter him. As our model for evangelizing, she always points to Jesus. Her truest desire, in union with all who evangelize, is to bring individuals either to their first real, personal encounter with Christ or to a deeper intimacy with him.

Mary shows us that being an effective witness to the gospel is not only a matter of "doing," but even more importantly, it is a matter of "being." We must first be a Christ-bearer. We must live "in Christ," or we cannot effectively bring him to others. And she shows us that this happens by grace. It is through God's grace that we can become so united with Christ in our very being that we manifest his presence in the world. We must take away the obstacles that impede the presence of God, and we must ask for that grace.

With Mary to Jesus

As we live in this age of the New Evangelization, we must consider how we can make the gospel of Jesus Christ compellingly attractive to men and women of our time. But we must first ask what makes the gospel so compelling to ourselves. And as we ask ourselves that question, we recognize that evangelization will always be a re-evangelization of ourselves, continually recovering and deepening our own faith.

We become evangelizers when people see in us something uniquely different than what they usually see in the world. When people see us living without the frantic acquisitiveness of our culture, living with spaces in life for stillness, living with a desire to continue learning, living with a kind of self-forgetfulness, and above all, living with a real and durable joy, people are naturally attracted by such a life, and they wonder why.

And we've got to learn how to tell them, so that their *why* leads to our *who*. We have to tell them who enables us to live without grasping, who leads us to seek stillness, who gives us a desire to keep learning, who shows us how to be generous, and who fills our hearts with joy. We've got to lead them to Jesus.

Our culture today is filled with people without hope, lives devoid of purpose, people seeking love in all the wrong places, people who have fallen away from the church and its sacraments because they never really found Christ there in a personal way, people who are seeking but they don't know for what they are seeking. Can we be people of the New Evangelization?

At Pentecost, the Holy Spirit came upon Mary and the disciples of Jesus, giving them the desire, energy, and courage to take the gospel to the streets of the world. The Holy Spirit turns the church from an inward-focused people and opens the church to its mission. The same Spirit who came to Mary that she might become the bearer of the Word of God, also fills us so that we may become bearers of God's word to the world. Let us look to Mary and ask for her maternal intercession in order to be like her: reflecting on the word of God, keeping that word in her heart, truly loving her Son, and radiating his love in the darkness of the world.

For Reflection or Discussion

1. What does Mary teach you about listening and witnessing to the word of God in her Annunciation and Visitation?

2. How does Mary's Magnificat demonstrate that she is Woman of the Word and also the first evangelizer?

3. What aspects of Mary's example can help you in your practice of lectio divina?

4. How is the star a fitting metaphor for Mary's work in the New Evangelization?

5. How can you, like Mary, become a Christ-bearer so that you can bring him to others?

6. What makes the gospel so compellingly attractive to you? How can you better express this to others?

7. How can you change from an inward-focused Christian to an outward-focused believer in Jesus Christ? How can you better respond to the questions of people seeking genuine faith?

OTHER BOOKS BY STEPHEN J. BINZ

AVAILABLE FROM OUR SUNDAY VISITOR